SURF
UK

SURF
UK

Wayne Alderson

fernhurst
BOOKS

British Library Cataloguing in Publication Data
A catalogue record for this book is available from the British Library

ISBN 1 898660 09 3

Acknowledgements

I would like to thank all the following for their help, advice and assistance with SURF UK:
Clive and Dawn, Nick and Joy, Roger and Ann in Newquay, Andrew Perry, Christopher
Billingham, Den and Barri, Martin Corr, Roger Castle, 'Medium sized' Trev, Paul
Knowles, Richard Harvey and Stevie, Chris Reed, Nick Noble and Gary Rogers of
Saltburn Surf Shop, Mark Axelby, Andy Bennetts, Colin 'The Caveman' Coventry, Billy
Cowie, David Long, The Gill, Andy 'Reg' Rendall, Tony Jeffs, Spout, John 'Jonno' Sirett,
Des at the Echo, Tim Bugler, Brian Southern, Nick Sime of Ma Sime's Surf Hut, Gul
Wetsuits, The Boys from Tyddewi and my parents, to whom this book is dedicated.

Cop out notice!

Neither the publisher nor the author accepts responsibility for accidents, drownings, drop-
ins or declarations of war arising as a result of information contained within this book.

Photographs

All photographs by Wayne 'Alf' Alderson except the following:
Cover photograph by The Gill. Nick Lloyd pulling a hard bottom turn at Skirza, NE
Scotland.
Page 1, Alex Williams, courtesy of Wave Graffiti.
Pages 43, 47, 141, Rick Abbott.
Page 82, Andy Moore.
Pages 98, 119, 120, 123, 135, 138, The Gill.
Page 103, Andy Bennetts/Camera Visions.
Page 118, Albert Tatlock.
Page 132, Caroline Mumby.

Many thanks to all the above photographers for their help

DTP by Alison Cousins
Illustrations by Michael Murray & Alison Cousins
Printed and bound by Ebenezer Baylis & Son Ltd, Worcester
Text set in 9pt Garamond (medium)

CONTENTS

FOREWORD

by Carwyn Williams, Former European, British and Welsh
Surfing Champion

Surfing isn't just a sport, it's a way of life - OK, that may be an old cliche, but it's true all the same and nowhere more so than in Britain where it really has to become part of your life if you're to make the most of it.

With ever-changing weather, winds and tides, only those who're in the know can make the most of the surf when it's pumping and this guide should help you do just that.

BUT, show some respect when you visit a new area - it goes a long way to making sure everyone has a good time in the surf and show a little respect for the ocean too. Leave the beach as clean as you found it - better still, leave it cleaner and join Surfers Against Sewage and get involved in the campaign to clean up Britain's beaches.

Whatever you do though, enjoy the surf. As a surfer you're privileged to enjoy something that very few people ever experience - the simple pleasure of riding waves.

Pages 2-3: Carwyn in action. Photo courtesy of Simmons/ Wave Graffiti

INTRODUCTION

I have done my utmost to make this Guide as accurate as possible - most of the information was gleaned from fellow surfers during a 10-week round Britain surfari. Much additional material has been gathered over the phone and by letter and included where applicable. Some people will disagree with certain facts, others will perhaps know of a spot that's not mentioned (although they're hardly likely to make a fuss about it), but a few hard-core surfers may take issue with me for revealing some of their 'secret' spots.

I must admit I had to think long and hard about mentioning certain places, but I came to the conclusion that, by now, the only secret spots left were either so difficult to get to, or in such surfing 'backwaters', that revealing them just wasn't going to have the crowds arriving in droves at some break that is only reached after a four mile route march and abseiling down a cliff.

For most surfers, the information within these pages will probably provide more than enough options. For those who want solitude, there are pointers in some chapters to where you may well find additional, but less accessible waves.

Detail on the landscape, culture, history etc of the different areas covered in the guide is intentionally limited - this is a surf guide after all. If you want to know more about an area than just the quality of the surf, you'll find a whole heap of guide books that are more than adequate for that purpose. So, let's surf....

Wayne 'Alf' Alderson, St. Davids, Pembrokeshire.

HOW TO USE THIS GUIDE

Much of the following may seem painfully obvious, but it might help you to get a better understanding of the guide if I briefly go through the way in which it was put together.

First, the layout of the chapters.
I've started with England, and perhaps not surprisingly Cornwall, because it's the most popular area in the country as far as surfing is concerned. From there the Guide takes you eastward through Devon, along the south coast of England, then up the east coast.

This is followed by Scotland, described in an anti-clockwise direction, from the east coast at the Borders, up to the north coast, along to the west coast, and back down. The Outer and Inner Hebrides are also covered in the section on the west coast.

Next is Wales, described in a clockwise direction, from east to west along the south coast, then up to the north west coast.

Each break is described under the headings Surf, Access, Facilities and Accommodation.

Surf Type of wave, size and direction of swell required for it to work, any notable characteristics of the wave (fast and hollow, slow and dribbly, etc.), best stage of the tide to surf, offshore wind direction and/or other winds it may work on, any hazards (rips, rocks, marauding sharks and canoeists, etc.), and suitability for beginners.

An invaluable document for any area is a tide table, which could make all the difference between whether you catch a break at the right time or not. Tide tables for the year are usually available at newsagents in each area. The times of low and high tide can also be found in most local newspapers.

Access Most beaches are given a grid reference before the description of the surf, based on the Ordnance Survey 1:50,000 Landranger Series (the relevant map number is also given). In a lot of cases grid references aren't entirely necessary, but I've still included them, just for the sake of attention to detail.

There are instances where there's no grid reference, or even Landranger number - this is in the case of beaches which just about everyone has heard about, such as Fistral.

With most breaks, a good road map will get you to them without too much difficulty. I used the Reader's Digest 'Atlas of the British Isles' during my travels, and found it more than adequate for the majority of beaches. However, the more remote beaches, especially in parts of Scotland, will probably require a map as detailed as the Landranger series to make absolutely sure you don't end up going round in circles, or find yourself on the wrong side of a rivermouth break.

The rest is easy enough - it consists of fairly straightforward details on the roads, footpaths and cliff scrambles you'll need to travel on or negotiate to get to each break.

You can assume that on most beaches you'll have to pay to use car parks between May and September, but you may find that parking is free in more remote areas.

Facilities Where the information was available, this section includes details on refreshment facilities available at or near the break, whether it's patrolled by lifeguards, nearest surf shops (where applicable), and in some cases, a few ideas for things to do after you've surfed, or if it's flat.

Accommodation This is simply very basic information on what's available locally in the way of caravan, camp sites and youth hostels. Information on B&B acccommodation is included in the Appendix.

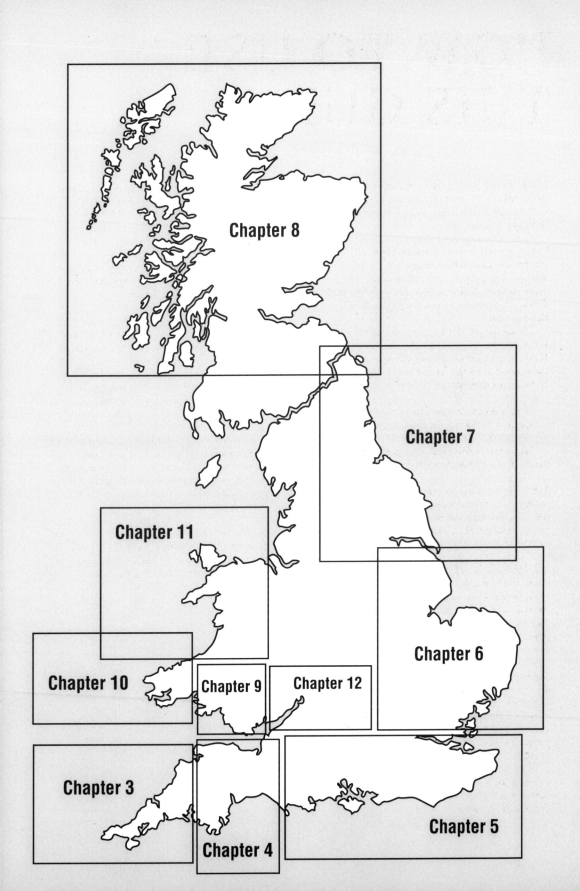

CORNWALL

NORTH COAST

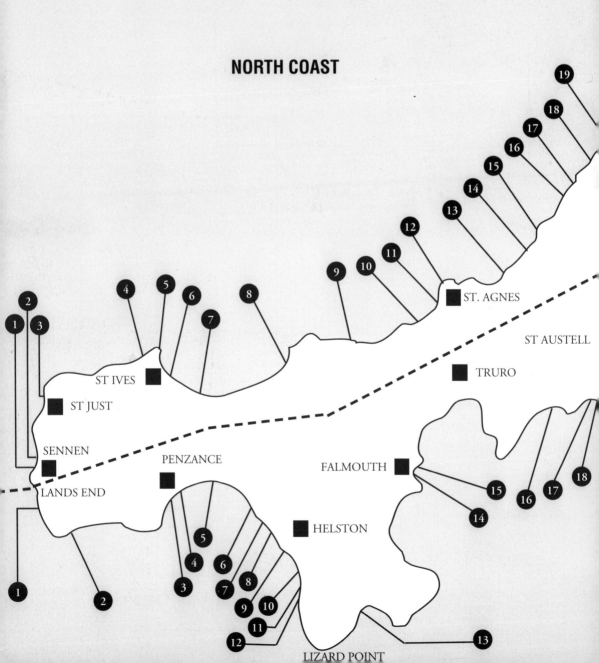

ST. AGNES

ST AUSTELL

ST IVES

TRURO

ST JUST

SENNEN

PENZANCE

FALMOUTH

LANDS END

HELSTON

LIZARD POINT

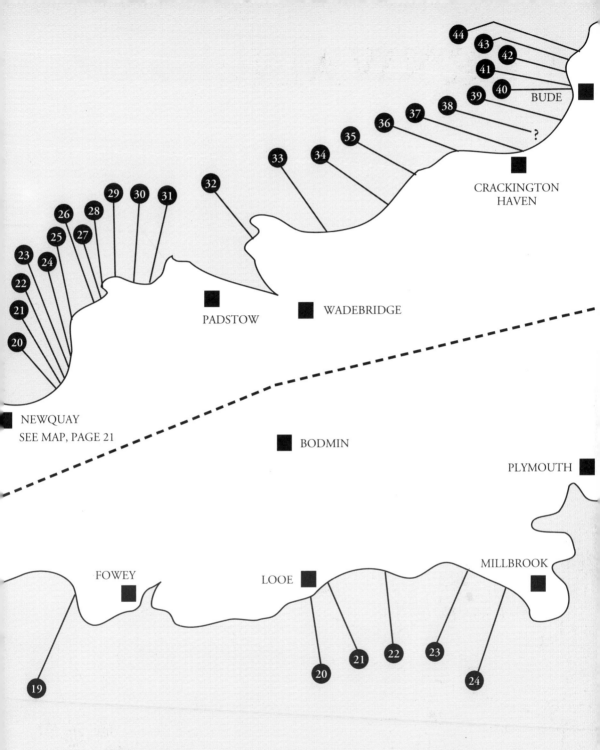

44
43
42
41
40 BUDE
39
38
37
36
35
34
33
32
31
30
29
28
26
27
25
24
23
22
21
20

?

CRACKINGTON
HAVEN

WADEBRIDGE

PADSTOW

NEWQUAY
SEE MAP, PAGE 21

BODMIN

PLYMOUTH

MILLBROOK

FOWEY

LOOE

19

20

21

22

23

24

SOUTH COAST

3 CORNWALL

Cornwall is undoubtedly the home of British surfing, with Newquay very much being the hub around which it all revolves. This is where 'Malibu' boards were first introduced to the country in the early 60's by visiting Australian lifeguards.

As far as the surf is concerned, Cornwall is ideally situated to pick up North Atlantic swells. Whilst these unfortunately lose some of their power as they move shoreward due to the British Isles' long continental shelf, the Cornish peninsula is still well exposed to virtually any swell going. It also has the advantage of having a coastline that consists of a mixture of beaches, cliffs, coves, inlets, and headlands facing in all directions.

Cornwall has, arguably, the biggest and most consistent surf in England. This, along with air and water temperatures that are the mildest in Britain has led to Cornwall becoming the focal point for what's happening on the British surfing scene - and it's a situation that seems unlikely to change much in the future.

CLIMATE

Year round surfing in Cornwall is no problem. Warmed by the Gulf Stream, and with warm but moist prevailing SW winds, water and air temperatures rarely, if ever, get unbearably cold.

That's not to say it doesn't get chilly in winter though. At this time of year the average air temperature is about 7°C (45°F), with water temperatures as low as 8-9°C (46-48°F). You'll need a winter steamer, boots, probably gloves, and possibly a hat - depends on your threshold of tolerance. Obviously not idyllic conditions, but winter has the advantage of producing the most consistent and powerful surf.

Spring gives a gradual rise in both air and water temperatures so it's not unusual to see people wearing summer steamers by mid-May, and you can also get some deep lows in the Atlantic being held at bay by high pressure over the UK, producing excellent surf and weather.

Summer sees the surf drop and the temperature rise. Average air temperatures are around 21°C (70°F), but it can, and frequently does, get a lot warmer. Water temperatures will vary from 13°C (55°F) in early summer up to 18°C or more (the mid sixties) in late summer if the weather's been

good. Surf is generally small, but the odd impressive swell comes through now and again. However, this is the holiday period, so as soon as the surf picks up, every man and his dog will be in the water, particularly at popular spots such as Newquay.

You won't need anything more than a summer steamer at this time of year, and on sunny days a spring suit may well suffice - even board shorts if it's really hot.

Late summer into autumn has the best surf, and the additional advantage that the crowds will have thinned as the holiday season draws to a close. Water temperatures are at their highest, air temperatures are still pleasant, and the surf starts to pump through quite consistently from deep lows out in the Atlantic throughout the autumn. Often the lows are still tracking well north, having little effect on the weather but giving day after day of clean, powerful ground swells.

As it gets later into autumn, temperatures obviously fall, and by early October you'll be thinking of getting out the winter steamer again, to be gradually followed by the boots, gloves, and hat as the New Year approaches.

You'll find once you're in Cornwall that local TV and radio stations provide regular surf reports for the area throughout the week.

One final point worth noting about Cornwall is that it's compulsory to have insurance to surf on some beaches here. Lifeguards can provide you with details.

Some sort of wave will usually occur from any low pressure system below 992mb in the North Atlantic - obviously the lower the better. If this coincides with high pressure over the British Isles you can expect the perfect combination of clean groundswell and offshore winds. The north coast is more exposed to these swells and thus has more consistent surf than the south Cornwall coast.

For convenience Cornwall is divided into two sections - north coast and south coast, with an arbitrary dividing line between the two at Land's End. The north beaches are numbered from 1 - 44 and the south beaches are numbered from 1 - 24.

NORTH COAST

1 SENNEN COVE
➤ *Landranger 203 GR 357265*

Surf The most south westerly surf beach in the UK, and one of the most consistent breaks in Cornwall on account of its exposed location, although the adjoining beach of Gwenver is usually bigger. A WNW facing beach break, with left and right-hand peaks up and down its length. Picks up any swell going, and tends to be best from low to mid tide. It's affected by shifting sands, which can vary the stage of the tide at which it works best.

Best in SE or E winds, which are offshore. Can hold a good-sized swell, up to around 8 feet and may have a wave when everywhere else is pretty flat.

A good place for beginners and experienced surfers alike, as the waves tend to increase in size as you move north up the beach, so you can choose the size of wave you feel happiest with. Watch out for rips though, especially at low tide.

Access To get there take the A30 towards Land's End, then right on a minor road in Sennen village and down the steep hill to Sennen Cove.

Facilities Car park above beach. Lifeguards in summer. Surf board hire, cafes, and hotels above beach. A surf school operates from Sennan, see appendix.

Accommodation Caravan parks and camp sites in Sennen and Crows-an-Wra. Youth Hostel at Kelynack, just outside St. Just.

2 GWENVER BEACH
➤ *Landranger 203 GR 363275*

Surf To the north of Sennen around Aire Point. A beach break, giving fast, punchy lefts and rights, which tends to work better at low and mid tide, but it's affected by shifting banks. At the N end of the beach there's a fickle right hander, breaking on a sand and rock bottom, which is best around low-mid tide. It picks up more swell than any other beach in Cornwall, so if it's flat here it'll be flat everywhere else. SE to E winds are offshore. OK for beginners, but beware of rips at the north end of the beach.

Access Either walk from Sennen Cove along the beach - about a mile - or drive back up the hill from the Cove and take the minor road to Escalls, where you'll find a car park above the beach at Tregiffian Farm. It's not easy to find without a detailed map. The car park is a couple of hundred feet above the beach - good fun running down the sand dunes to the surf; hard work coming back up afterwards.

Facilities There are no facilities at Gwenver other than the car park.

Accommodation See Sennen.

3 PRIEST'S COVE
➤ *Landranger 203 GR 352317*

Surf This is a right-hand point break which works on swells from SW to north. SW to SE winds are offshore. Not recommended for beginners as there are no lifeguards here.

Access Take A3071 into St. Just, a narrow lane leads from St. Just to the cove.

Facilities Car park above beach. Occasionally an ice cream van. Toilets in car park. Nearest shops in St. Just.

Accommodation See Sennen.

4 PORTHMEOR
➤ *Landranger 203 GR 516410*

Surf This is a small beach at the N end of St Ives. A beach break giving peaks which vary as the tide changes. Low-tide produces a fast, hollow wave which has a tendency to close out, particularly if the wind is onshore. At mid-tide there's a better wave giving longer rides, while high-tide produces well-shaped peaks and a heavy shorebreak on the inside.

The peaks shift around, although there's a pretty consistent right-hander off the 'island' at the E end of the beach. There's also a peak known as The Boiler; so named after an old ship's boiler half-buried in the sand. This is a fast, heavy, hollow wave breaking in shallow water. It more than often closes out, but if you're into taking off, pulling in, and getting tubed for three or four seconds before being nailed, it might just suit you. It's popular with spongers.

There's a rip running from left to right along the beach, but it can be a hard paddle out on a big day as there's no longer an obvious rip available to help you out. Picks up swell from SW to N, southerly winds are offshore. Not suitable for beginners at low tide. Popular with the St. Ives locals.

Access   In summer it's not worth the hassle of trying to drive through town to the beach just park as near as you can and walk. In the off-season you might be able to park closer.

Facilities   There are lifeguards in summer, and plenty of shops and cafes nearby, plus public toilets.

5 THE BREAKWATER, ST. IVES
➤ *Landranger 203 GR 523410*

Surf   As the name implies, this wave breaks off the breakwater in front of St. Ives harbour. A long, often hollow, left-hander. It needs a big swell to work, and is affected by ever-shifting sands. When the swell gets really huge it can be one of the only surfable waves on the north coast - and on these occasions it may get crowded simply because there's nowhere else to surf. Best from low to mid-tide. Southerly winds are offshore.

Access   May be difficult in the summer

Facilities   Shops, cafes and public toilets. Lifeguards in the summer

North Cornwall coast

6 HAWKS POINT
➤ *Landranger 203 GR 534388*

Surf   A left hand beach break breaking off rocks to the W end of Carbis Bay. Needs a big swell to work, and produces a wave right through from low to high tide. It tends to work when everywhere else is closed out. SW winds are offshore here. Watch out for rips. OK for beginners but be aware of the the rips. Note that there are no lifeguards.

Access   Difficult to get to - there's no adjacent parking, so you have to walk down the cliff path. You can also get there from Lelant, but it's a long hike through the golf course by the church and along the beach.

Facilities   None.

7 HAYLE
➤ *Landranger 203 GR 548384*
GWITHIAN TOWANS
➤ *GR 570400*

Surf   Hayle is a river mouth break. Watch out for currents from the river Hayle flowing out to sea.

Winds from SW to SE are offshore.

If it's no good here, there are peaks throughout the long stretch of beach immediately NE of Hayle. The beach faces NW, and consists of miles of smooth sand backed by low cliffs, with sand dunes behind. The break works best from low to threequarters tide. Be careful not to become trapped against the cliffs at high tide. Best on S to SE winds. Beginners, especially, should beware of rips on big swells.

Access and Facilities To get to the break at Hayle, take the minor road out to Riviere Sands caravan cark just NE of Hayle town. There's parking above the beach/rivermouth. As well as a pub there are shops on the camp site. If these are closed the nearest facilities are in Hayle.

For Gwithian Towans, take the B3301 out of Hayle and turn off at the sign for the village. This road has speed bumps. There's a big car park above the beach, and a shop and take-away on the opposite side of the road.

Accommodation There are two more caravan parks and camp sites besides Riviere Sands just south of Gwithian at Phillack and Black Cliff.

8 GODREVY TOWANS / RED RIVER
➤ *Landranger 203 GR 580420*

Surf At the northern end of St. Ives Bay. A right-hand beach break at low-tide, with a left at mid tide. It holds swells up to about 8 feet, but it is very exposed, so any winds other than light SE-E tend to spoil things.

As with the breaks further south, watch out for rips on a big swell. Apart from this, OK for beginners.

Access From the car park at Gwithian, you walk up to the beach through the dunes.

Facilities The nearest shops are in Hayle.

Accommodation Caravan parks and camp sites beside Riviere Sands south of Gwithian at Phillack and Black Cliff.

9 PORTREATH
➤ *Landranger 203 GR 654455*

Surf There are two breaks here, a beach break in the centre of the bay, and a steep, fast, and tricky right-hand reef break off the harbour wall which works at mid-high tide. This one is best left to experienced surfers only. Watch out for rocks here.

Badlands tube

Opposite top: Bashing a Badlands lip
Opposite bottom: Perran Sands

Above: Waiting for the swell, North Cornwall

SE/S winds are offshore, but it also works in a south westerly wind.

Access On B3301 from S, or B3300 from N, both of which take you to outskirts of the village from where you'll easily see the road to the beach.

Facilities Big car park above the beach, with cafes and shops, and public toilets, plus board and wetsuit hire at 'Long John's'. Lifeguards in summer.

Accommodation Nearest camping and caravan sites are just inland on B3300, or at Porthtowan.

10 PORTHTOWAN
➤ Landranger 203 GR 691482

Surf A good left and right-hand beach break which works all through the tide. Best on an incoming tide. Best in E to SE winds. Beware of rips at low-tide, otherwise safe for beginners.

Access To get there, from S take signposted minor road off B3300, from N take signposted minor road off B3277. If travelling along A30, follow signs to Porthtowan from Scorrier.

Facilities There's a big car park at the beach and public toilets. There are plenty of shops and cafes, plus a pub, 'The Commodore'. The beach is patrolled by lifeguards in summer. Popular watering holes with surfers include Nelson's Bar, and Bruce's Bar and Nightclub.

Accommodation Nearest camping sits and caravan parks are inland just off the B3300 or at Porthtowan.

11 CHAPEL PORTH
➤ Landranger 203 GR 697497

Surf One of the most consistent beaches in Cornwall, it picks up more swell than most of its neighbours. It's also very 'typically Cornish', with abandoned tin mines on the cliffs overlooking the beach.

A beach break with peaks all over. It can get pretty hollow at times. The peaks tend to move about as the banks change shape regularly. Best from mid to low tide. At high tide the sea hits the cliffs on either side of the cove, so be careful. In the cove itself backwash from the cliffs spoils the wave. Best in a SE to E wind. This area is known as The Badlands by the locals. It's a good idea to show respect when surfing here, or you'll probably find out where the name came from.

Access   Access from the N is down a steep, narrow, and twisty road, signposted from the B3277 just as you come out of St. Agnes, or from the Porthtowan - St. Agnes road, following the signs carefully.

Facilities   Big car park above the beach, cafe and toilets in summer. Also a stream running down the side of the car park which is useful for rinsing off your wetsuit.

Accommodation   Caravan parks and camp sites between Porthtowan and Perranporth.

Droskyn Ward, Perran Sands

12 ST. AGNES
➤ Landranger 203 GR 722518

Surf   St. Agnes is a beach break that works best on an incoming tide from mid to threequarters tide, but beware of rocks on the inside. On a big SW or W swell it's often the only place in the area that is still surfable, one reason being that it's sheltered from SW winds. It can hold big waves up to 10 feet or more.

Access   Take the B3277 from the A30 into St. Agnes (narrow, twisty streets and a steep hill, so drive carefully) then follow signs to the beach. Alternatively come in from the N on the B3285 to Peterville, and once again follow signs.

Facilities   There's a car park above the beach, plus pubs, cafes, surf hire, and lifeguards in summer. (Local surfers are often to be found in the 'Driftwood Spars', particulary on Friday and Saturday nights when a band may be playing. And there's Harry's Wine Bar up the hill in Peterville). There's also a local surf shop where hire equipement is available. See Appendix.

Accommodation   There are plenty of caravan parks and campsites between Porthtowan to the S and Perranporth to the N.

13 DROSKYN POINT / CHAPEL POINT
➤ *Landranger 203 GR 753544*

Surf Left hand point break to south of Perranporth beach, breaking towards the mouth of the River Perran. Can hold a good-sized wave, but at high tide there's a problem from backwash off the cliffs and submerged rocks. Watch out for rips. SE to E winds are offshore. Not a beginners wave.

Access From the main beach at Perranporth it's a short walk or drive to the cliffs above the break, from where you can check it out.

Facilities Car park above the break, also next to beach in Perranporth. Plenty of shops, pubs, and cafes in Perranporth, toilets at beach car park. Popular pubs include the Green Parrot and the Beach Wine Bar - literally on the beach at Perranporth.

Accommodation There are plenty of caravan parks and camp sites around Porthtowan, particularly as you head north towards Newquay.

Perfect summer surf, North Cornwall

14 PERRANPORTH
➤ *Landranger 200 GR 755545*

Surf A popular beach break that generally works best from mid to high tide, with peaks throughout its length. These shift around a lot as the sandbanks move. Tends to get crowded, and there can be bad rips and currents, so beginners should be careful. SE to E winds are offshore. Lifeguards in summer.

Access Perranporth is well signposted from the A30 and easily reached. There's a big car park directly in front of the beach.

Facilities See Droskyn Point(13).

Accommodation See Droskyn Point (13).

15 PERRAN SANDS / PENHALE
➤ *Landranger 200 GR 760570*

Surf A two miles long beach stretching N from Perranporth with left and right-hand peaks throughout its length. Picks up a lot of swell and is well worth a visit when the surf is not working too well elsewhere. The beach is so long that if you're prepared to walk you can usually find an uncrowded

wave somewhere. The peaks vary as the sandbanks shift. The waves are often slow, so it's a good place for beginners, but beware of rips which are often very strong. A long, hard paddle out on a big swell. Works at all stages of the tide.

There's also a very good right-hander in Penhale corner at the N end of the beach, but it's a long walk. If you're walking up from Perranporth, watch out for quicksands at low tide! It needs very calm conditions or a light easterly to work best as it's very exposed. There's a good rip along the cliffs taking you out to the break. This is the only place in Britain where I have seen a shark while surfing!

Access The S end of the beach can be reached by walking up from Perranporth. To reach the quieter peaks further N, and Penhale corner, drive to the Warner Holiday Camp about two miles N of Perranporth on the coast road. You're allowed to drive through the camp and park at the top of the dunes above the beach. There's a superb view from the top of the dunes as they're about two hundred feet high, and the descent to the beach is good fun. But it's a different story coming back up after a long session in the water! The dunes above the N end of Penhale Sands are part of a MoD range, and access may be restricted when they're firing.

Facilities There are shops in the holiday camp in summer, otherwise the nearest comprehensive

facilities are in Perranporth. If you intend going for the day take food with you, as the climb up the dunes on a hot day just for a sandwich is not a prospect to fill anyone with joy.

Accommodation The holiday camp itself is one option, with caravans and chalets well situated above the beach. Alternatively there are numerous caravan parks and camp sites in the area.

16 HOLYWELL BAY
➤ *Landranger 200 GR 765595*

Surf A somewhat erratic NW facing beach break, with left and right-hand peaks that can work at all stages of the tide, but tend to be best at mid to high tide. On a big swell you may also get a left off Gull Rocks to the S of the beach at low-tide. Beware of rips at low-tide. SE winds are offshore. OK for beginners.

Access There's a signposted road off the A3075 to Holywell, and a path from the village along the side of the stream to the beach.

Facilities Lifeguards in summer. Parking, shops, pubs and toilets are all available in the village. The Treguth Inn is popular with surfers.

Accommodation Numerous caravan parks and camp sites in the area, particularly as you head towards Newquay, six miles north.

17 PORTHJOKE
➤ *Landranger 200 GR 770607*

Surf A beach break that only works at low tide when it can give a good right-hander. Works in winds from S through to E. Not ideal for beginners.

Access Take the turn-off from the A3075 to Crantock-West Pentire-Porthjoke. Park in car park next to the Bowgie Inn, and walk down lane to beach. The Bowgie Inn and Nightclub is popular with local surfers.

Facilities Nothing on the beach itself, the pub is the nearest place for food and drink, otherwise nearest shops etc. are in Crantock.

Accommodation Plenty of caravan parks and camp sites.

18 CRANTOCK
➤ *Landranger 200 GR 785610*

Surf A sheltered NW facing beach backed by sand dunes, with the river Gannel flowing along the N side. This beach often remains surprisingly quiet when Newquay's beaches are heaving with surfers.

There's a fast, sucky right-hander at low tide on the right of the beach, and on a big SW swell a good left-hander breaks on the left of the beach at low to mid tide, best on an incoming tide.

Best in a SE wind, but also relatively sheltered from strong NW and SW winds.

Safe for beginners unless the swell gets big - patrolled by lifeguards in summer, so take their advice if in doubt.

Access Follow signs to Crantock from the A3075. The Gannel can be crossed from Newquay by either ferry or tidal bridge at Fern Pit or Trethellan. There's a lane from Crantock village through the dunes to a car park above the beach. It's quite a long walk from here to the surf. You can also park at Pentire Headland, where a path leads from West Pentire to steps down the cliff.

Early summer swell, Fistral

Facilities Toilets in both car parks, nearest shops, cafes, and pubs are in Crantock and West Pentire.

Accommodation See Newquay.

19 NEWQUAY

And so to the mecca of British surfing, Newquay. This is where surfing first took off in Britain, and it is still the focal point of almost all new developments in the sport - board, wetsuit, and clothing design all tend to hit Newquay first.

There are probably as many surf shops and equipment manufactures per square mile around Newquay as almost anywhere in the world, so if you're surfing in this area you can rest assured you'll never have to worry about getting hold of spares or replacements.

In summer the whole place goes crazy - the streets are jammed with vehicles, every other one with a board on the roof; the beaches are packed, and out in the water it can be wall to wall fibreglass - this definitely isn't the place for those who like to surf alone. August sees the peak of the action as the competition season gets under way, with ASP rated events attracting the world's top surfers to Fistral, one of the most consistent - and crowded - beaches in Britain.

All this surf hype has resulted in a large and often talented surf population in the town - some of Britain's best surfers are based in Newquay, so the competition for waves can often be pretty fierce.

Newquay has the great advantage having a variety of beaches, all within close proximity, facing in different directions from W through to NW and N. This means that as long as there's a swell running, the chances are that one or more of the beaches will pick it up.

In describing Newquay's surf, I've included an additional section at the end on 'Facilities and Accommodation' rather than repeat the same thing for each beach.

Newquay's beaches are taken to include Fistral, Towan, Great Western, Tolcarne, and Lusty Glaze. The latter four are known collectively as the 'Bay Area'. All are within easy reach on foot from the town centre.

FISTRAL

You're hardly likely to need a grid reference to find Fistral, Britain's best known surfing beach - when there's a good swell, just follow the crowds. Fistral is the spot where competition and pro surfing came of age in Britain. On a good day it can produce fine, powerful, beach break waves: it also has the advantage of picking up more swell than most other beaches.

However, as its fame spread, the crowds increased. Now you'll have to get up very early in the morning to get the place to yourself, especially when there's a good swell coming through.

The breaks at Fistral, from S to N, consist of South Fistral, North (or Main) Fistral, and Little Fistral.

SOUTH FISTRAL

Surf   A mainly left hand beach break over a rock and sand bottom. Best from mid to high tide, it can give long rides, although the take off area can be very crowded. When the wind is cross-shore at North Fistral, Pentire headland gives this wave good protection from the wind.

A good-sized wave can be surfed here on a big swell - when it's big here you can save yourself a hard paddle out by jumping off the rocks halfway along the headland. NOT recommended for beginners. S to SE winds are offshore.

Access   If you're driving, take the B3282 on the one way system through Newquay and follow signs to Pentire from the top of the town. You can park above the beach and walk down.

Facilities   The main cafe is at the other end of the beach at North Fistral along with toilets, cold showers, and lifeguards. There are also toilets above the beach at South Fistral.

NORTH FISTRAL

Surf   The best spot in the area when the banks are right. However, as with so many beach breaks, they're subject to constant change. Best at low tide, when it can produce quality tubing waves and good peaks. On a big swell it will work at all stages of the tide. Predominantly a right hander, but lefts are to be found too. Take care if surfing left around high tide as you'll be riding into an area of submerged rocks and rip currents. The rights in particular can give good long rides.

At high tide there's a sucky, dumping shore break caused by the steeply shelving beach, this can make paddling out difficult.

A good swell here may produce 6ft - 8ft waves for three or four days in a row, especially in winter. This is potentially a good break for beginners because it is well-patrolled by lifeguards in the summer, but beware of the crowds and above all observe the golden rule - DON'T DROP IN! Best on a S'ly wind.

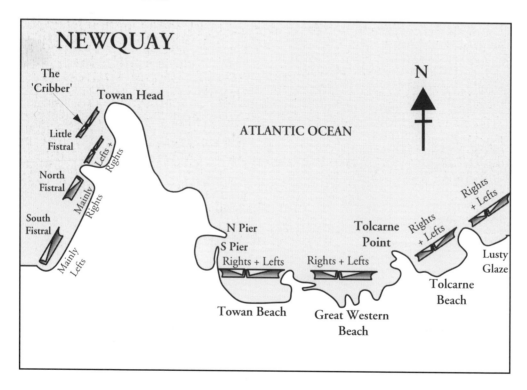

Access The beach is well signposted, but on a good swell all you need to do is follow the crowds. Parking all along the road and above the beach. If you can drive all the way to the beach in August - particularly when one of the surf contests is on - you deserve at least one good wave to yourself.

Facilities Big cafe above the beach, also toilets and showers. Lifeguards are based at this end of Fistral.

LITTLE FISTRAL

This is the small bay to the immediate north of North Fistral which is exposed at low tide, which is when it works. It can be a good left and right hand beach break if the banks are right. Keep an eye out for the incoming tide or you may find yourself doing a lot of rock-hopping when you paddle back in. For this reason it's not really recommended for beginners. SE winds are offshore.

Access Either walk from North Fistral, or you can drive out to Towan Head and park above the bay. Facilities Toilets above the bay, otherwise see North Fistral.

Going for take off, Fistral

THE CRIBBER

Just to prove that Newquay is the 'complete' surf spot, it has it's own big wave, the Cribber. It breaks off Towan Head, out past Little Fistral. The Cribber requires a very big swell to work, when it may produce double-overhead waves or bigger. Understandably, it's not often ridden, and as with all big waves it's surrounded by myth and legend.

It goes without saying that a wave like this should be attempted by only the most competent surfers. Apart from the sheer hazard of the size of the Cribber, the surfer must be able to cope with strong currents. There is also the the fact that once you're up and riding, you're surfing straight in to the rocks of the headland - so a bad wipeout can have serious consequences.

Access and facilities See Little Fistral.

THE BAY AREA

This consists of Towan, Great Western, Tolcarne, and Lusty Glaze beaches, which become just one long beach at low tide. As all of them face in a N to N-W'ly direction, S to S-E'ly winds are offshore, and they're all well protected from the prevailing S-W'ly winds. The quality of the waves will vary depending

22 WATERGATE BAY
➤ *Landranger 200 GR 840650*

Surf   Watergate Bay has two miles of beach at low tide, so if it's crowded in Newquay this is a good option - a walk up or down the beach should bring you to a relatively uncrowded peak. The waves are all beach breaks, both lefts and rights, and it works all the way through from low to high tide, although it can become crowded at high tide as it's one of the few places locally that works at this stage of the tide. The breaks vary as the banks change. S - E'ly winds are offshore. A good beginner's wave if the swell is not too big.

Access   On the B3276 Newquay - Padstow road, well signposted. Car park at top of beach - if that's full there's another further up the road.

Facilities   Toilets in car park, well stocked cafe with board hire, pub opposite car park. Lifeguards in summer.

Accommodation   Plenty of camp sites locally and around Newquay.

23 BEACON COVE
➤ *Landranger 200 GR 844688*

Surf   A low tide beach break with good lefts and rights, but needs a good sized swell to work. Best in a SE or E wind. Not a beginners wave due to difficulty of access.

Access   Difficult. On the B3276 about five miles north of Newquay and half a mile south of Mawgan Porth. Look out for a track leading to the Beacon, and take this to the cliff edge (not in your car). From here there's a pathway which weaves its way 200ft or so down the steep cliff.

Facilities   None on the beach, the nearest are at Watergate.

Accomodation   There are caravan parks and camp sites. Youth hostel at Treyarnon.

Right: Surf to Save contest, Polzeath, picks up a clean autumn groundswell
Below: Small but fun, Constantine Bay

24 MAWGAN PORTH / TRENANCE
➤ *Landranger 200 GR 849675*

Surf   Left and right hand beach break, with a good left-hander at the south end of the beach. Best from low to mid tide. It picks up a lot of swell and doesn't usually get too crowded. Best in SE or E winds. OK for beginners, although there are rips to be wary of at times.

Access   On the B3276 mid-way between Newquay and Treyarnon. There's a car park above the beach. Walk through the dunes to the surf.

Facilities   Shop and garage in Mawgan Porth. Lifeguards on the beach in summer. The Traveller's Rest is a popular pub.

Accommodation   Caravan and campsites and limited B&B locally, otherwise try Newquay or Padstow. Youth Hostel at Treyarnon.

26 BEDRUTHAN STEPS
➤ *Landranger 200 GR 849695*

Surf   A low tide break with peaks that tend to be

somewhat lacking in power, but have the advantage of being well sheltered from the wind. SE to E winds are offshore. There are sometimes rips at low tide, and you should also beware of the incoming tide which breaks against the cliffs at high tide - for these reasons not recommended for beginners.

Access   There's a car park off the B3276 north of Trenance, from where there are steps down the cliff to the beach. The beach is owned by the National Trust, as is the car park. It's part of a superb stretch of coastline consisting of towering cliffs and golden sands with rock stacks dotted here and there. The legend is that the rocks were used by a giant, Bedruthan, as stepping stones - hence the name.

Facilities   Toilets in the car park, and a National Trust shop and a cafe near the car park.

Accommodation   As for Mawgan Porth.

26 TREYARNON BEACH
➤ *Landranger 200 GR 858740*

Surf   Treyarnon can produce some quality surf, with a nice left-hand point break off the rocks on low tide as well as left and right hand peaks on the beach itself. There's also a sand-covered reef break at Treyarnon Point, giving low tide rights and lefts on almost any swell. Best in SE and E winds. The beach itself is OK for beginners.

Access Take the signposted minor road off the B3276 into Treyarnon, where you'll find a car park above the beach.

Facilities There's a shop in the car park, plus shops in Treyarnon itself. Lifeguards patrol the beach in summer.

Accommodation Caravan parks and camp sites locally, plus a youth hostel to the right of the beach.

27 CONSTANTINE
➤ *Landranger 200 GR 858748*

Surf Constantine picks up a lot of swell, and provides a mixture of beach and reef breaks, with a good left hander to the south of the beach. There are right and left hand peaks on the beach itself, and a high tide left over the rock projection between Constantine and Booby's to the north. Best in S-SE winds. However, there are strong cross currents and eddies on the beach, so it's not really recommended for beginners on bigger swells.

Access About a mile north of Treyarnon by road. From Treyarnon turn left, then left again down to the beach. There's a car park by the beach - walk through the dunes to get to the breaks.

Facilities Shops in the village.

Accommodation See Treyarnon.

28 BOOBY'S
➤ *Landranger 200 GR 858755*

Surf Picks up most swells to produce left and right-hand beach breaks, with a good right-hand reef break, The Slab, at the northern end of the beach on a big swell. S-SE winds offshore. Not really a beginner's wave due to strong rips.

Access About 10 minutes' walk north of Constantine.

Facilities None.

Accommodation See Treyarnon.

29 HARLYN BAY
➤ *Landranger 200 GR 825757*

Surf A N-E facing beach, so the prevailing S-W winds are offshore here. Needs a good swell to work best, when it can give some really good beach break waves and a good right hander off the main rock on the beach. Best from low to mid tide, although it will work through to high tide. It's a popular wave with the locals. OK for beginners.

Access Left off the B3276 on to a minor road which runs along the SE corner of the beach just before coming into Padstow from the south. Car park above the beach, footpath from car park.

Facilities Pub just above beach. Other refreshment available close to beach in Harlyn village. Toilets in car park. Lifeguards patrol the beach in summer.

Accommodation Caravan parks and camp sites around Treyarnon or in Padstow. Youth hostel at Treyarnon.

30 NEWTRAIN BAY
➤ *Landranger 200 GR 885758*

Surf A low tide beach break, also with a good right-hand reef break on a reasonably sized swell.

Access Newtrain Bay is situated midway between Harlyn and Trevone, and reached by footpath from either.

Facilities None.

Accommodation See Harlyn.

31 TREVONE BAY
➤ *Landranger 200 GR 889761*

Surf Just around the corner from Newtrain, Trevone is a right and left-hand beach break which is best at low tide on a three to six foot swell. SE winds are offshore. OK for beginners.

Access Take the minor road signposted to Trevone off the B3276 just east of Padstow.

Facilities Limited refreshments available in village.

Accomodation See Harlyn.

32 POLZEATH (HAYLE BAY)
➤ *Landranger 200 GR 935795*

Surf (see diagram) Polzeath, or Hayle Bay, whichever you prefer, has a variety of breaks to suit just about everyone. It also picks up most swells, and although the waves may not be renowned for their speed, they often have well-shaped slow peeling walls which are great fun to surf. There are surfable waves at low tide (one hour before low water to two hours after), consisting of a classic right-hand reef with a shorter left breaking between Pentire Point and New Polzeath. The main beach break (lefts and rights) is in the middle of the bay, and a slower left-hander to the south west. It's often at its biggest close to low water.

At high tide there's a similar set up further up the beach, with a good right hander breaking below New Polzeath, lefts and rights off the beach break peak in the middle of the beach, and a slower left below Tristram Cliffs to the south.

SE to E winds are offshore, but it's also sheltered from NW winds. The bay is safe for beginners, but watch out for rips at low tide.

Access From Wadebridge take the B3314 and follow signs to Polzeath. The road from Polzeath to Trebetherick runs above the beach, and there's a car park next to it which has direct access to the beach.

Facilities Cafes, shops, surf shops (see Appendix) and pubs above the beach.

Accommodation Caravan parks and camp sites on the cliff top and in Tredrizzick, Padstow, and Wadebridge. The White Lodge Hotel in Polzeath welcomes surfers.

The beach is extremely popular with holidaymakers of all varieties, so don't expect to get it to yourself.

33 PORT ISAAC
➤ *Landranger 200 GR 995809*

Surf A small beach which can produce a beach break with lefts and rights at low tide. SW-SE winds are offshore/cross-shore.
Access Take the B3267 from the B3314. It leads straight into the harbour (not literally), where there's limited parking.

Facilities Limited facilities.

Accommodation Nearest camp sites are at St. Minver and Delabole.

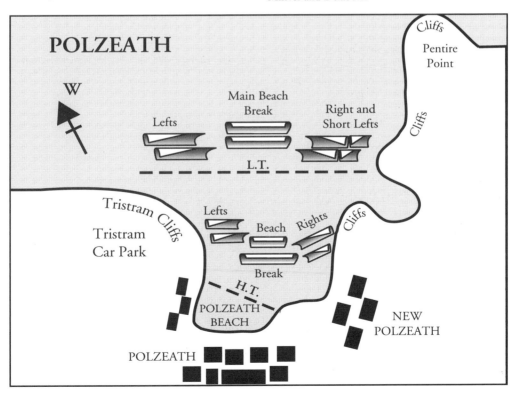

34 TREGARDOCK
➤ *Landranger 200 GR 040842*

Surf A beach break with lefts and rights that picks up most swells. Works from low to three-quarter tide. SE to E winds are offshore. Not suitable for beginners.

Access Turn NW off B3314 just south of Delabole and follow signs to Treligga. There's a turn-off to Tregardock just before Treligga. It's a long walk from here to beach.

Facilities None.

Accommodation Camp sites at Dalabole and Bossiney. Youth hostels just up the coast at Tintagel and Bossiney.

35 TREBARWITH STRAND
➤ *Landranger 200 GR 048876*

Surf A popular local break, this is a beach break with lefts and rights. At high tide the waves break against the cliffs above the beach - as a result it's best surfed from low tide, on an incoming tide. SE to E winds are offshore. Relatively safe for beginners, but keep an eye on the tide.

Access Take the B3263 off the B3314 just north of Camelford. Trebarwith village is signposted down a minor road, follow this through the village to a car park and picnic site above the beach. Trebarwith can also be reached via signposted minor roads off the B3314 at Delabole.

Facilities Shops and pub in village.

Accommodation See Tregardock.

36 BOSSINEY HAVEN
➤ *Landranger 200 GR 068906*

Surf A somewhat fickle low tide beach break, with both lefts and rights, which can be good occasionally. It faces NW so there's more chance of catching it on a swell from a northerly direction. SE winds are offshore.
Access On the B3263 to the NW of Delabole and Camelford. The road goes through the village, with a steep hill on the southern side. There's a short walk from Bossiney village to Bossiney Haven down a steep cliff path.

Surf to Save, Polzeath

Facilities   Refreshments available in Bossiney and Tintagel.

Accommodation   See Tregardock.

37 CRACKINGTON HAVEN
➤ *Landranger 190, GR140970*

Surf   Typical Cornish cove, with a narrow sandy beach flanked by steep cliffs on either side. A low tide beach break, both lefts and rights. Beware of rocks on either side of the beach, particularly at the southern end. OK for beginners. SE to E winds are offshore.

Access   Reached by minor roads from either the A39 at Wainhouse Corner or the N end of the B3263. Steep roads to village, where there's a small car park, often full in summer. From here it's a short walk to the beach.

Facilities   Shop, cafe, and toilets in village. Lifeguards in summer.

Accommodation   Camp sites outside the village and a youth hostel at Bossiney.

38 SECRET SPOT
➤ *Landranger 190*

Surf   Just a few little clues about this spot, although most locals will no doubt readily identify it. It's somewhere between Boscastle and Widemouth and is a classic reef break when it works - and it's not really all that 'secret'.

39 WIDEMOUTH
➤ *Landranger 190 GR198020*

Surf   A long sandy beach with cliffs at either end, Widemouth is a very popular surf spot, so you may find it very crowded. It has good left and right hand beach breaks along its length. There are waves at all stages of the tide, with a good left-hander at the S end of the beach from low to mid tide, and a right-hand reef break from mid to high tide. E winds are offshore.
A good beach for beginners, but beware of rock outcrops in various parts of the bay, and don't paddle out from the N end of the beach in a large swell, as the waves can push you back into the cliffs and rocks.

Access   Either take the minor roads off the A39 signposted to Widemouth, or the coast road from Bude and Crackington which runs through Widemouth. There's a large car park right at the beach.

Facilities   Refreshments available above the beach. Surf hire is available, and the beach is patrolled by lifeguards in summer. There are a number of surf shops in Bude (see Appendix).

Accommodation   Caravan parks and camp sites just outside Widemouth, particularly to the south, and in Bude. There are also a number of hotels if your funds stretch that far.

40 SUMMERLEAZE, BUDE
➤ *Landranger 190 GR 203067*

Surf   The beach to the north of the river mouth, Summerleaze often works when the adjacent beach, Crooklets, and nearby Widemouth are closed out. Bude is the largest coastal town in this part of Cornwall, so the surfing population is correspondingly large. However, there are plenty of less crowded breaks either side of Bude if you're prepared to drive.
   Summerleaze needs a good-sized swell to really work properly, partly because the river Bude flowing out to sea has a tendency to flatten out smaller swells, partly because it's protected to an extent by the harbour wall. It's a beach break, with the waves breaking on sand bars. There is also a right off the rocks by the swimming pool at high tide. The rocks can be used by experienced surfers as a means of getting out through the waves as the tide comes in on bigger days. Best on an incoming tide, although it will work at all stages of the tide. SE to E winds are offshore. OK for beginners.

Access   From the A39 take the A3072 into Bude and follow signs for the beach. Plenty of parking near the beach, although it's always crowded in summer.

Facilities   Lifeguards patrol the beach in summer - in fact Bude is where the first surf life saving club in the UK was formed in 1953, by an Australian, Alan Kennedy. Shops, pubs, etc. all readily available in the town. There are several surf shops in Bude (see Appendix).

Accommodation   Plenty of camping and caravan sites around Bude and Widecombe.

41 CROOKLETS
➤ *Landranger 190 GR 203072*

Surf Immediately north of Summerleaze, past the swimming pool - it's only a short walk between the two. The break here varies depending on the sandbanks, but it can have good lefts and rights. The rights are by the rocks to the north end of the beach, and are best at low tide. There's a left at high tide which works all through the tide, but is generally better on a rising tide. At high tide watch out for the backwash off the rocks. There's also a rip to the north. Apart from these two hazards, fine for beginners. E'ly winds are offshore. As the beach has a tendency to close out, it tends to be better on a smaller swell.

For access, facilities etc see Summerleaze.

42 NORTHCOTT MOUTH
➤ *Landranger 19 GR201085*

Surf Really an extension of the beach at Bude, as are Sandy Mouth and Duckpool further north. This is a low tide beach break producing both rights and lefts. At high tide the sea comes right up to the cliffs, so be careful not to get trapped. E winds are offshore. OK for beginners as long as it's not too big a swell, when bad rips develop. Keep an eye on the incoming tide.

Access Take the Flexbury to Poughill road out of Bude. At Poughill you'll find signs to the beach. Parking above the beach.

Facilities Cafe at beach in summer.

Accommodation There's a camping and caravan site in Poughill.

43 SANDY MOUTH
➤ *Landranger 190 GR 202099*

Surf Beach break with lefts and rights, this stretch of coastline seems to pick up most swells. Worth a visit if Bude is too crowded or closing out.

Conflicting views over the best stage of the tide - some say it's best at low, others at mid tide. At high tide the waves break over the rocks to be found at the top of the beach - watch out for these. The beach is so exposed that the waves only really have good shape on light E'ly winds or calm conditions. Even cross-shore winds can make a real mess of the surf. On a big swell there are strong rips. For this

reason, and the danger from submerged rocks, it's not a particularly good break for beginners.

Access Follow signs from the A39 to the beach. There's a National Trust car park from where you take a path and steps down to the beach.

Facilities Cafe in car park in summer.

Accommodation See Bude.

44 DUCKPOOL
➤ *Landranger 190 GR 200116*

Surf A beach break, both lefts and rights, best on an incoming tide from low to mid tide. As with Sandy Mouth, there are submerged rocks at high tide, and it's best with a gentle E wind or no wind at all. There may be bad rips on a big swell. Not a good beach for beginners.

If the waves are no good on this stretch of coastline, there is some fine coastal walking, with sheer cliffs and small rocky coves. The Coombe Valley just inland also offers some pleasant walks.

Access From the A39 follow signs to Coombe Valley - Duckpool is at the end of the valley (it's signposted). Car park above the beach, from where you walk down to the break.

Facilities Cafe by car park in summer.

Accommodation See Bude.

SOUTH CORNWALL

The south of the county is predominantly a winter surf zone - it needs the larger swells of winter to work well, as it lacks the north coast's exposure to the Atlantic. However, a good-sized swell at any time of year may produce a wave at certain spots; Porthleven in particular, which is one of England's best reef breaks. When a N or NW wind is blowing out most of the north coast and there's a big swell running, this is the place to head for.

The south coast is rather more mellow than the north. It has fewer dramatic cliffscapes, and more secluded coves and wooded inlets - a far more pastoral landscape, with some lovely beaches, such as Caerhays, where the fields and woods come down almost to the water's edge.

As with the north coast I've started from Land's End and worked east.

1 NANJIZAL
➤ *Landranger 203 GR 357237*

Surf   Not often surfed due to difficulty of access, but it apparently has a good beach break at low tide on a big swell. It needs winds from N to E to work best (the beach faces SW). Not recommended for beginners because it's very isolated.

Access   Not easy - you'll need an OS map to find it - it would take too long to give detailed descriptions. You can drive all the way to the beach down a dirt track, depending on how much you value your suspension.

Facilities   None

Accommodation   Nearest caravan parks and camp sites are at Sennen. Youth hostel at St Just.

2 PORTHCURNO
➤ *Landranger 203 GR 389223*

Surf   A good low tide beach break, with lefts and rights, the lefts being particularly good. A low tide break, with low spring tides the best. Needs a big swell and a NW wind to work properly.

Access   From the B3315 turn south at Trethewey and follow signs. Drive through the village to a large car park about 100 yards above the beach.

Facilities   Cafe in summer, otherwise there's a pub and shops close by in the town. The unique open air theatre on the cliffs above the beach is really worth a visit.

Accommodation   There's a camp site at nearby Treen, otherwise see Nanjizal.

3 NEWLYN
➤ *Landranger 203 GR 466286*

Surf   A good right-hander breaks off the harbour wall, often hollow. It needs a very big SW swell to

The long and the short of it

work, but works well in strong SW and W winds that blow out many north coast breaks. Best from mid to high tide. Not recommended for beginners.

Access   Take the main road through Newlyn and you can't miss it. Plenty of parking space above the beach.

Facilities   Shops, cafes, pubs in Newlyn. Mousehole, just to the south of Newlyn is a picturesque Cornish fishing port which is well worth a visit.

Accommodation   See Nanjizal. Camp sites in nearby Penzance, and a youth hostel.

4 PENZANCE
➤ *Landranger 203 GR 478306*

Surf   A beach break that faces south, thus requiring a very large swell to work. There's also a right off the pier on a good swell. It's OK in a strong W wind, although offshore conditions are more to the NW'ly.

If you're a surfer with a partner you may have to juggle your time

OK for beginners.

Access   Take the main A30 into Penzance - it runs alongside the beach. There are plenty of car parks in the vicinity, with a large one on the quay.

Facilities   Penzance is the main town in this part of Cornwall, and has all the facilities you might require, including a number of surf shops.

Accommodation   Camping and caravan sites and a youth hostel.

5 MARAZION
➤ *Landranger 203 GR 515307*

Surf   Another beach break, with lefts and rights, once again requiring a big swell to work. A long, crescent shaped beach. OK for beginners. N to NE winds are offshore.

Access   On the A394 some three miles east of Penzance. Best access to the beach is just after the railway bridge on the bend above the beach as you come from Penzance. There's a car park above the beach.

Facilities Cafe near the car park, but not much else unless you go into Marazion or Penzance. One thing you can't fail to notice here is St. Michael's Mount, the 17th century castle perched on the island out in Mounts Bay. At high tide the island is cut off from the mainland and can only be reached by boat, but at low tide there's a causeway across to it.

Accommodation Caravan parks and camp sites. See Penzance.

6 PERRANUTHNOE
➤ *Landranger 203 GR 540292*

Surf Picks up more swell than the beaches to the W, although nearby Praa Sands is better still. It still needs a good sized swell from the W or SW, when it can give a worthwhile beach break wave, both lefts and rights. Worth a visit when the north coast is blown out, as it works in N'ly winds. OK for beginners, but watch out for rocks dotted around the cove. Best from mid to high tide.

Access On the A394 two miles E of Marazion, turn off right for the village and the beach. There's a car park above the beach.

Facilities Cafe above the beach.

Acommodation Plenty of caravan parks and camp sites around Marazion and Praa.

7 KENNEGY COVE
➤ *Landranger 203 GR 563283*

Surf A beach break needing a large SW to W swell to work. Best from low to mid tide. It will continue to work in a strong W or NW wind, although N winds are offshore. Not recommended for beginners.

Access Take the minor road off the A394 to Kennegy Cove, park here, and take the coast path down to the cove.

Facilities None at the beach.

Accommodation Caravan park and camp site at Kennegy, also see Praa Sands.

8 PRAA SANDS

Surf A mile-long SW facing beach which has left and right-hand beach breaks up to around 6ft on a good-sized W to SW swell, which can give fast and hollow waves. It can work in summer, although it's far better in winter, when it's probably the most consistent beach on the south coast west of the Lizard. It tends to be better from mid to high tide on an incoming tide. At high tide it may start to close out. Best in a N-E'ly wind but will also work in a N-W'ly . OK for beginners, but watch out for a rip at low tide.

Access Take the minor road off the A394 to the beach, which is signposted.

Facilities At the west end there is a car park, public toilet, cafe, the Welloe Rock Inn and a surf shop. At the other end of the beach is another large car park.

Accomodation There are numerous caravan and camping sites locally, plus accomodation in holiday flats right above the beach.

9 PORTHLEVEN
➤ *Landranger 203 GR 625255*

Surf One of the best reef breaks in England, which works on a good, solid SW swell or a very large W swell. Porthleven can throw up a wave both summer and winter, although as usual with the south coast, the break is usually better in winter.
It's a fast, hollow and very shallow right hander, which gives a relatively short but excellent ride. Tube rides are definitely in order here. It works from around 4ft - 12ft, and is best around mid tide. As the tide drops you should watch out for the inside bowl section, which can suck dry. Don't try surfing here at high tide - you'll be too close to the cliffs, and a wipeout could have dire consequences. There's also a backwash to contend with.
It has to have a N to NE wind to work. As should be apparent from the description, this is definitely only a break for experienced surfers. It doesn't hold a crowd. Strong rips on a big swell.
The long narrow beach to the SW also has a beach break - an alternative if the reef is looking a little too daunting or crowded.

Access Porthleven is directly SW of Helston, off the A394 on the B3304. There's a limited amount of parking around the harbour.

Facilities Shops, toilets, pubs, etc. around the harbour.

Accommodation Nearest caravan parks and camp sites are at Helston or Praa.

10 GUNWALLOE
➤ *Landranger 203 GR 654224*

Surf A beach break, with lefts and rights breaking on to a pebbly beach backed by low cliffs - really an extension of the beach at Porthleven. Needs a big SW or W swell to work. NE winds are offshore. OK for beginners if the swell isn't too big.

Access Take the A3083 south out of Helston, and turn right at turn-off to Berepper. You can park above the beach at Berepper, which is at the S end.

Facilities None

Accommodation Caravan site just outside Berepper. Otherwise it's back towards Helston for camping and caravan sites.

11 CHURCH COVE
➤ *Landranger 203 GR 662205*

Surf A picturesque little cove which gets it's name from the 15th century church of St. Winwaloe just above the beach. It needs a big swell to work, when it can give left and right hand beach break waves. Best from low tide on an incoming tide - at high tide most of the beach is under water. There's a rip at low tide to watch out for, otherwise OK for beginners.

Access Continuing on the coast road from Berepper, Church Cove is just to the south over the hill. From Helston take the A3083 south, turn off for Cury just north of Cross Lanes. Once you reach the golf course above the beach drive straight into it and follow the road, which later becomes a dirt track, over the hill and through the course to the cove - short cuts across the greens are not in order! Park in grassy dunes above beach.

Facilities None

Accommodation There are campsites at Mullion and Predannack to the south, and a caravan site north of Berepper.

12 POLDHU COVE
➤ *Landranger 203 GR 664199*

Surf Another scenic south coast beach, with a beach break on big SW and W swells. Best towards low water on an incoming tide. NE winds are

offshore. Quite sheltered from S and N winds. OK for beginners, but there are rips to be wary of at low water. The beach can get quite busy in summer.
Access From Church Cove, take the road through the golf course, then directly over the hill to the south. From Mullion take the minor road to the NW to the beach. Car park close to beach.

Facilities Beach cafe, toilets, lifeguards in summer. Quite an historic spot - it's from here that Marconi made his first radio transmissions across the Atlantic, and nearby Dollar Cove is named after the coins that were washed up on to the beach after a ship wreck in the days of sail - perhaps there are still some there to be found?

Accommodation See Church Cove.

13 KENNACK SANDS
➤ *Landranger 204 GR 735165*

Surf Two beaches which join together at low tide. This has beach breaks up and down it's length and needs a huge swell to work. As it faces SE it may also pick up rare SE to E swells. NW winds are offshore. A popular family beach in summer, so may be busy. OK for beginners.

Access Turn E off the A3083 Helston-Lizard road at Ruan Major and head for Kuggar. There's a car park above the beach.

Facilities Cafes and toilets above beach.

Accommodation Caravan parks and camp sites in Kuggar, Ruan Major, Mullion and Coverack (which also has a youth hostel).

14 MAENPORTH (FALMOUTH)
➤ *Landranger 204 GR 791297*

Surf At the south end of Falmouth, this is a beach break which works on a very big SW or W swell, or after a strong easterly wind has been blowing. NW winds are offshore. Can be crowded in the surf, and on the beach. OK for beginners. A good place to head for when the north coast is onshore or too big.
Access Car park above beach, although it may not be easy to reach in summer traffic.

Facilities Falmouth has all you're likely to need in the way of shops, cafes, and pubs, and the beach is patrolled by lifeguards in summer. Surf shops in the town.

Caught inside, Cornwall

Accommodation There are plenty of caravan parks and camp sites around Falmouth's outskirts.

15 GYLLYNGVASE BEACH (FALMOUTH)
➤ *Landranger 204 GR 809316*

Surf A left and right hand beach break, and there's a reef break here too. As with Maenporth it works on a big SW or W swell, or after a strong easterly has been blowing. It's a good option if the north coast is too big or blown out. NW winds are offshore. Can get crowded at times. OK for beginners.

Access Car park above beach. Access may be difficult in summer, but it's unlikely to have surf then.

Facilities See Maenporth.

Accommodation See Maenporth.

16 PENDOWER BEACH
➤ *Landranger 204 GR 900380*

Surf A very picturesque and sheltered cove in Gerrans Bay, with a beach break that requires a very big swell to work, so you're most likely to catch it at its best during the winter. N to NW winds are offshore.

Access From the A3078 the minor road to Carne takes you to a National Trust car park above the beach.

Facilities Toilets in the car park. The Pendower House Hotel Cafe overlooks the beach.

Accommodation The nearest camp sites are at Veryan Bay to the N and St. Just-in-Roseland to the S. There is a youth hostel at Boswinger.

17 CAERHAYS / PORTHLUNEY COVE
➤ *Landranger 204 GR 975413*

Surf A reasonably consistent break by south coast standards, this is a beach break which once again requires a very big swell to work, preferably in conjunction with N'ly winds, which are directly offshore. It can hold waves up to about 6ft when it's working, and it works at all stages of the tide. OK for beginners.

Caerhays has plenty of character, situated as it is at the end of a lush wooded valley with steep, tree-lined cliffs on either side and a Victorian castle overlooking the beach.

Access From the A3078 follow signs down twisting minor roads to St. Michael Caerhays, from where a lane runs S down to the beach. There's a car park just above the beach.

Facilities Toilets in the car park. A beach cafe in summer.

Accomodation Camp sites and caravan parks around Boswinger and Portholland. There's a youth hostel in Boswinger.

18 PENTEWAN
➤ *Landranger 204 GR 019467*

Surf A long sandy beach with left and right hand beach breaks, which tend to be better towards the middle and S end of the beach. As it faces SE it would presumably pick up swell from strong easterly winds as well as from those from the south west. Best from low to three-quarter tide. At high tide it has a tendency to close out. NW winds are offshore. OK for beginners.

Access Directly S of St Austell on the B3273. There's a large caravan park and camp site above the beach with a car park in front of the beach.

Facilities Shops, toilets, etc. at the camp site, although how many of their facilities you can use will depend on whether your staying there or not. Shops, pubs, etc. are also available in the picturesque harbour of Mevagissey a couple of miles to the S, or in St. Austell.

Accomodation The caravan park and camp site above the beach is most convenient, but there are a number of others in the area. There is a youth hostel in Boswinger.

19 POLKERRIS
➤ *Landranger 204 GR 093521*

Surf A beach break which tends to be rather dribbly as the beach is shallow. Needs a big SW or W swell. Best on an incoming tide. Northerly winds are offshore. The area is often covered in a veil of white dust from the nearby china clay works. OK for beginners.

Access From the A390 north east of St. Austell take the A3082 to Fowey, then follow the signs along the minor road south to Polkerris. Parking above beach.

Facilities Shops and pub in Polkerris, while nearby St. Austell is the main town in the area and has all the associated facilities.

Accommodation Camping and caravan site between Polkerris and Par, off the A3082. Youth hostel at Golant to the north.

20 LOOE
➤ *Landranger 201 257533*

Surf On a very big swell there's a beach break here, plus a right off the harbour wall at high tide. OK in winds from a northerly quarter. Suitable for beginners.

Access The A397 runs through Looe, but the town is an attractive fishing port and very popular with tourists, and the narrow streets are closed to non-resident traffic, so access can be difficult. You can't park near the beach, so be prepared for a walk from car parks on the outskirts of the town.

Facilities Plenty of shops, pubs, and cafes in the town.

Accommodation There are caravan parks and camp sites scattered around the area.

21 MILLINDREATH
➤ *Landranger 201 GR 296540*

Surf A high tide beach break, giving lefts and rights. Offshore in a W'ly wind. Tends to be bigger than nearby Looe, and has easier access.

Access Turn off the B3253 at Great Tree for the beach. Parking above beach.

Facilities Limited refreshments available locally.

Accommodation Caravan park and camp site at Great Tree. Also see Looe.

22 SEATON
➤ *Landranger 201 543304*

Surf Left and right hand beach breaks which require a bigger swell than the nearby breaks in Whitsand Bay. Best at low to mid tide. W to NW winds are offshore. Just to the E is DOWNDERRY, which has some good reef breaks and is well worth checking. The beach is OK for beginners (but watch out for rips), the reefs are best left to experienced surfers.

Access From the A387 turn south on the B3247 which takes you into Seaton. The road runs above the beach and along to Downderry and Whitsand Bay. Park above the breaks.

Facilities Shops and pubs in Seaton and Downderry.

Accommodation Nearest camp sites and caravan parks are around Looe.

23 PORTWRINKLE
➤ *Landranger 201 538360*

Surf A SW facing beach situated in the three-mile sweep of Whitsand Bay, with high but gently sloping slate cliffs above the beach. This area is popular with surfers from Plymouth, the biggest city on the SW coast and only about five miles away. Left and right hand beach breaks, best at low tide. Watch out for rocks at high tide. N to N-E'ly winds are offshore. OK for beginners, but there are strong rip currents to be wary of, particularly on a big swell. Pollution can be a problem here at times.

Access The B3247 runs along the cliffs above Whitsand Bay. There are a number of turn-offs on to it from the main A374 to the N, which connects with the ferry to nearby Plymouth at Torpoint. There's a car park overlooking the break, and a path from here down the cliffs to the beach.

Facilities Public toilets on the beach. There's a cafe on the cliff top and another at the bottom of the cliffs. Lifeguards patrol the beach at weekends in summer. Shops and pubs in Portwrinkle, which is a popular holiday town.
   Plymouth has whatever you can't find locally, and also has good road, rail, and sea links with the rest of the UK and Europe. For surfers coming to SW England from the continent Plymouth has daily sailings to and from Roscoff in Brittany and Santander in Spain.

The A38 dual carriageway from Plymouth connects with the M5 to Bristol and all points N and E, including Wales.

Accommodation Caravan and camping site at Tregonhawke at the W end of the bay, otherwise they're all around the Looe area. There's also plenty of reasonably-priced accommodation, plus a youth hostel in Plymouth.

24 TREGANTLE
➤ *Landranger 201 GR 527386*

Surf Beach break with lefts and rights at all stages of the tide, but best at mid to high. When it works, one of the biggest waves in this area. Offshore in a N'ly wind. Beginners should beware of strong rips.

Access Take the road along the cliffs from Portwrinkle. There's a path down the cliffs at Tregantle, but the area around Tregantle Barracks is used as a firing range, so if a red flag is flying, access will be prohibited.

Facilities See Portwrinkle.

Accommodation See Portwrinkle.

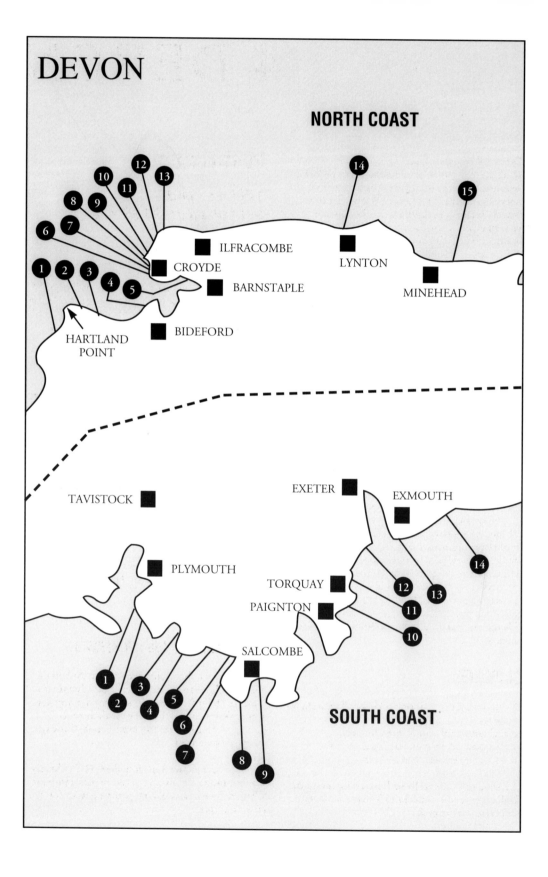

4 DEVON

Devon, like Cornwall, has surf on both its north and south coast, but it occurs under somewhat differing conditions on each of the two coasts. The north coast is by far the most consistent, with the best beaches generally being those that face due west and pick up plenty of swell from the Atlantic. These beaches work under much the same conditions as those of the north Cornish coast. The north facing beaches require bigger swells to work, but spots such as Lynmouth can produce excellent waves.

The south coast is like the south coast of Cornwall in that it requires a very big swell, typical of autumn and winter, to work, as the waves have to push a long way up the English Channel before they reach the Devonshire coast. For this reason surfing on the south coast is a rarity in summer apart from the occasional exception such as Bantham, which picks up more swell than other south coast beaches.

On the south coast there's a tendency for the swell to drop off markedly a couple of hours or so after high tide at many of the breaks, so as a general rule it's often best to surf here around high tide.

The north coast was where surfing in Devon first took off back in the 60s and 70s, and the area around Croyde and Braunton is now the centre of a thriving surf industry, which supports a number of equipment manufacturers, and several surf shops.

The Devonshire coastline, both north and south, is famed for it's beauty, varying from rugged, tree lined cliffs interspersed with small coves, to long sandy beaches backed by sand dunes and rolling hillsides where the farms produce the famed Devonshire clotted cream. Parts of the north coast are within the Exmoor National Park. There are good-sized towns close to most of the breaks, although the area to the west of Bideford is relatively isolated.

CLIMATE

Devon has a similar climate to Cornwall with almost identical air and sea temperatures throughout the year. Consequently, you'll need the same combinations of neoprene as suggested in the previous chapter when surfing here.

This chapter has been divided into two sections, the north coast (1-15) and the south coast (1-14). Both work from west to east.

NORTH COAST

1 SPEKE'S MILLS
➤ *Landranger 190 GR 225237*

Surf Speke's is a good quality reef break, with rights and lefts, often hollow, breaking over a rocky reef in the centre of the cove. It picks up just about any swell going, and can often have a small wave when everywhere else is flat. Paddle out to the left or right of the break to avoid the wave itself. Alternatively you can jump off the rock platform that projects from the southern end of the beach. E'ly winds are offshore. Not a beginners wave.

Access The most difficult thing about surfing at Speke's Mills is finding it. It would take too long to describe the route in detail, so invest in a good map or take directions from a local inhabitant. You should take a route through Hartland - Milford - Kernstone Cross - Docton Mill, from where there's a long, bumpy, narrow dirt track to the beach (if it's wet it may be as well to park on the hill at Kernstone Cross and walk the half mile or so to the beach).

Facilities None other than a lifebelt above the beach! The nearest village of any size is Hartland, which has pubs and shops - but not many.

Accommodation Youth hostel at Elmscott, and a caravan park and camp site at Hartland and Welcombe Cross.

2 CLOVELLY
➤ *Landranger 190 GR 319248*

Surf I had conflicting information on this break - some said it doesn't have a wave, others that there's a good beach break at low tide, so here's a chance for you to do some exploring for yourself instead of getting all your information from a book! Clovelly is worth a visit anyway.

Access Turn off the A39 on to the B3237. Clovelly is at the end of the road. You have to park above the village and make a steep and quite long walk down to the harbour.

Facilities   Plenty of tea 'shoppes', cafes, and 'taverns' in Clovelly. Devonshire cream teas and ice cream on sale everywhere!

Accommodation   Caravan park and camp site at Dyke and Buck's Mills.

3 BUCK'S MILLS
➤ *Landranger 190 GR 350243*

Surf   Buck's Mills needs a very big swell to work; but when it does it can produce a long, left-hand point break. The take off point tends to shift around a bit, and can be steep. The wave breaks alongside 'The Gore', a man-made pile of boulders that juts out to sea. It's best at a low spring tide, but will also work at other times when it's best just before low water. You have to clamber across and paddle over rocks to get out to the break. You will be surfing over rocks, so it's a break for experienced surfers only. Buck's Mills has the advantage of being the only break in North Devon that still has surfable waves on a SW gale. S'ly winds are offshore. E'ly winds, when strong, can ruin the surf.

Access   Follow signposts from the A39 to the village. Park in the village and walk to the break.

Facilities   Limited number of shops, etc, in the village.

Accommodation   Local cavaravan park and campsite.

4 WESTWARD HO!
➤ *Landranger 180 GR 432294*

Surf   A long NW facing beach break, with lefts and rights throughout it's length. Works all through the tide, but at high tide the far right of the beach is the only place with a decent wave. There are two low tide reef breaks to the left end of the beach; these are best left to experienced surfers, but the beach itself is OK for beginners. SE winds are offshore.
   Not much frequented by visiting surfers as it's some way from the main breaks around Croyde.

Access   The B3236 runs into Westward Ho! from the A39. Follow the one-way system around the town to the beach. There are car parking facilities above the beach.

Facilities   Cafes, shops, public toilets above the beach. Lifeguards in summer.

Accommodation   It's probably best to base yourself in one of the camp sites or caravan parks close to Croyde, although there are plenty locally. There is a youth hostel at nearby Instow.

5 CROW POINT
➤ *Landranger 180 GR 458324*

Surf   A rarely surfed rivermouth break in the mouth of the Taw and Torridge estuary. To work, it needs very big swells associated with a high spring tide. On the whole, this is a winter break. A point break wave breaks in front of the boardwalk through the dunes from the car park. It can only be surfed from about two hours before high tide through to high water. During this period, however, there's a very strong tidal current flowing up the estuary, against which it is almost impossible to paddle. Unless you want to be seen floating through Barnstaple on your board you're probably best advised to walk back along the beach to the break after each ride. It works best in calm conditions or light winds from N to E. Strong S or W winds ruin it. Not a beginners wave because of the strong current.

Access   Take the A361 out of Barnstaple, and turn off at Wrafton just before entering Braunton. There's a toll road from Velator to the car park in the dunes above the estuary.

Facilities   Nearest comprehensive facilities are in Braunton (see Croyde for details).

Accommodation   Plenty of caravan parks and camp sites.

6 SAUNTON
➤ *Landranger 180 GR 446370*

Surf   Saunton is one of the best waves in Devon for beginners, and also a good longboard wave, because the beach shelves very gently and produces slow waves which tend to re-form a number of times and are ideal for learning on. The beach is also over two miles long, so if you're prepared to walk a bit you shouldn't have any trouble avoiding crowds.
   By the rocks at the N end of the beach is a rip, which is a useful means of getting out to the line-up as long as you know what you're doing. There's also a right-hander which breaks just off the rocks around mid tide, although it needs a reasonably good-sized swell to work. There is also a left that breaks towards the rip.
   Saunton is offshore in an E'ly to S-E'ly wind, but is quite well sheltered from N'ly winds.

Croyde Bay

Access Take the B3231 out of Braunton. You can't miss the beach, and there's a large car park down on the left of the main road.

Facilities Lifeguards in summer. For more details see Croyde.

Accommodation See Croyde.

7 DOWNEND POINT
➤ *Landranger 180 GR 432385*

Surf A right hand point break that can give good long rides when it's working. It breaks over jagged rocks at the headland between Saunton and Croyde, and surfing here involves paddling out and coming back in over rocks; so it's definitely only for experienced surfers.

'The Point' needs a good sized swell to work at its best, and is best two hours either side of low water. After low tide a N'ly tidal stream starts to flow around the point from Saunton and makes it extremely difficult to stay in the line up, which in any case shifts about a lot.

There are two 'gullies' in the rocks through which you paddle out, the more northern being the better option. Getting back in can be more tricky than paddling out, so check the place out carefully before you surf it, and maybe even ask for advice from the locals. Getting caught inside is a sure way of getting the adrenalin flowing unless you're the kind of person who finds it easy to relax when faced with the prospect of being pounded on hard surfaces. Wetsuit boots are a good idea even in summer just in case you find yourself doing some involuntary rock hopping. Best in calm conditions or in a light E'ly wind.

Access Take the B3231 out of Braunton; Downend Point is the headland you go round after you pass Saunton on the left. There's limited parking available above the point.

Facilities None. See Croyde.

Accommodation See Croyde.

8 CROYDE BEACH
➤ *Landranger 180 GR 435393*

Surf   Croyde is the focal point of surfing in Devon, and the beach here is the most popular surf spot in the county - consequently it's also the most crowded. If you're just taking up the sport, or have limited experience, you'd be well advised to go around the corner to Seaton or Putsborough where you can learn without being hassled by anyone and without getting in the way of more experienced surfers.

Croyde has a reputation for having one of the best beach breaks in Britain, with fast, heavy, and hollow waves common around low water, especially on spring tides. The waves, which break both right and left, will continue to work all the way through the tide, particularly on bigger swells. There are usually a number of peaks up and down the beach, which will vary in quality depending on how the constantly shifting sand banks are aligned with the swell. On bigger swells, there's a good left-hander at the south end of the bay which works at around three-quarter tide. E'ly winds are offshore.

Access   The B3231 from Braunton leads into Croyde. At weekends and during holidays traffic congestion can be a problem, but there's plenty of parking at various points above or near to the beach. Car parks at Downend (closed in winter), and to the S of Baggy Point.

Facilities   Above the beach there are cafes and shops, plus board hire and toilets. The beach is patrolled by lifeguards in summer, who can have a major say in where you surf as it's their job to designate swimming and surfing areas. Croyde and Braunton both have adequate shopping facilities, including lots of surf shops with Braunton having the wider choice of the two.

Popular watering holes in Croyde include the Thatched Barn pub in the centre of the village, and the Ruda Park, a large camp site above the beach where there are plenty of associated facilities including a nightclub which is popular with both local and visiting surfers.

Accommodation   In addition to the Ruda, there are caravan parks and camp sites dotted around this stretch of coastline between Croyde and Ilfracombe to the north, which offer everything from organised chaos to quiet seclusion.

9 CROYDE REEF
➤ *Landranger 180 GR 428398*

Surf   A fast, right hand reef break. It builds very quickly and breaks in shallow water over rocks: very definitely a wave for experienced surfers only. It needs a sizeable swell to work, and is best just either side of high tide. SE winds are offshore. As with Downend Point, a pair of wetsuit boots are advisable here.

Access   From Croyde Beach take the minor road west out to the National Trust car park at Baggy Point (a popular rock climbing area). The car park is in front of the break.

Facilities   The nearest shops are at Croyde Beach or in the village.

Accommodation   See Croyde.

10 PUTSBOROUGH
➤ *Landranger 180 GR 448410*

Surf   A beach break with lefts and rights which has the advantage of being the only place in the area that is reasonably protected from winds from the S and S-W. It's best from about mid tide to high water, with the swell tending to increase in size as the tide comes in. At high tide there's a problem from backwash off the cliffs above the beach. On a big swell it can continue to produce good waves as the tide drops.

The waves at Putsborough are rarely of great quality and they break a long way out, which can make paddling out hard work. There is a rip by the rocks. Offshore winds are from SE to E.

Apart from the inevitable crowds when there's a SW or S wind messing up everywhere else, Putsborough is a very good beginners wave, as it's generally slower and more forgiving than Croyde. You can avoid the crowds too by simply walking for a few minutes down the beach and finding your own peak.

Access   From Croyde take the minor road north out of the village and up over the hill and down to Putsborough, following the signs. This is a typical Devonshire country lane - narrow, twisty, and hemmed in by high hedges.

From Woolacombe take the road south to Croyde and watch for signs to Putsborough at Georgeham - once again the roads are narrow.

There's a large car park on the cliffs above the beach which you have to pay for, but very little parking elsewhere.

Facilities There's a beach shop and a toilet block in the car park, otherwise the nearest shops etc. are in Croyde. The beach is patrolled by lifeguards in summer.

Accommodation The car park at Putsborough allows campervans to stay overnight - for a fee of course - but not tents. Otherwise see Croyde.

11 WOOLACOMBE
➤ *Landranger 180 GR 450430*

Surf A two mile stretch of beach from Putsborough to the south, with left and right hand beach breaks throughout its length. It works all the way through the tides. There's also a nice right hander off the rocks at the north end of the beach which works from mid to high tide. The best winds for this beach are from SE to E.

Woolacombe is big enough for you to be able to avoid crowd hassles by walking down the beach to a quieter peak. A good beach for beginners.

Access Take the B3231 from Croyde, following signs to Woolacombe. There's a turn-off to the left on to a minor road just south of Woolacombe which takes you to the town, and gives you a good view of the line-up as you drive down towards the coast. If you're coming from Braunton, take the A361 north, then left on the B3343 into Woolacombe. Car parking is available above the beach.

Facilities There are surf shops in the town, and plenty of cafes, pubs, and shops for apres-surf grub. Lifeguards patrol the beach in summer.

Accommodation There's heaps of holiday accommodation around Woolacombe - holiday villages, camp sites, caravan parks and hotels. There's also a youth hostel at Ilfracombe, just to the north.

Putsborough - grey and windy but the best bet on a south-westerly wind

12 BARRICANE
➤ *Landranger 180 GR 455445*

Surf   Known locally as Combesgate, Barricane is a
northward extension of Woolacombe beach at low
tide, but becomes isolated from it by a rocky
headland at high tide. This is another beach break
with short lefts and rights, but it's only really a low
to mid-tide break, as there are rocks all over the
place at high tide. It's sheltered from N'ly winds by
high ground to the N; but as with Woolacombe, it's
easily spoiled by S'ly winds. Offshore winds are from
the E. Not a beginner's wave.

For Access, Facilities, and Accommodation   see
Woolacombe.

13 GRUNTA BEACH
➤ *Landranger 180 GR 454447*

Surf   To the N of Barricane, this is a beach break
which works at low tide, and can produce some
pretty good lefts. E'ly winds are offshore.
Woolacombe would be a better place for
inexperienced surfers than Grunta.

Access   On the Woolacombe-Mortehoe coast road.
Park above the beach.

Facilities & Accommodation   See Woolacombe.

14 LYNMOUTH
➤ *Landranger 180 GR 723496*

Surf   A north-facing bay which works far less
frequently than the neighbouring west-facing
beaches. Lynmouth has two excellent left hand point
breaks, and a fast, hollow right hander when there's
a big swell running.
   The best of the left handers is to the W of the
mouth of the river Lyn - it's generally bigger and
faster than the other, and works best from low tide
to a couple of hours or so before high water.
   The other left, also to the W of the river mouth,
is a low tide wave which is slower but longer: rides
in excess of 400 yards are possible on a good swell.
   The right is to the E of the river mouth, and
starts to work at high tide. It's a fast, hollow wave,
breaking into the river mouth. On a big swell this
can work right through the tide.
   Lynmouth is best in calm conditions or in a light
S'ly. Strong S W or S-E'ly winds, even though not
onshore, can mess it up. Even strong southerly

winds have a tendency to eddy in the bay and spoil
the shape of the waves.
   This is a break for experienced surfers only. You
will be paddling out and surfing over submerged
boulders, and, as the tide rises, there are obstacles
such as marker poles to avoid. In addition you will
be surfing towards the harbour wall. Note that there
are also strong rips.
   Lynmouth will only work on a BIG swell - if it's
overhead, say 8ft or more on the west facing beaches
and the winds are light S to SE, there's a good
chance Lynmouth will be working. It's best surfed
on an incoming tide.

Access   Lynmouth is just off the A39 north coast
road - it's well signposted. You go down a steep
(1:4), thickly wooded valley to the beach. Lynmouth
itself is a very scenic spot.

Facilities   There are plenty of shops, car parks and
cafes within easy reach of the beach.

Accommodation   There are a number of camping
and caravan sites around Lynmouth, plus a youth
hostel in Lynton.

15 PORLOCK WEIR
➤ *Landranger 181 GR 865480*

Surf   This is actually in Somerset, but there are too
few breaks in that county for it to warrant a chapter
to itself. It's a left-hand reef break, fast and hollow.
It's best two hours either side of high tide. It needs a
very big swell to work, but may be worth a visit if
everywhere else is too big. S to SW winds are
offshore. Not a beginners wave. At low-water
pollution can be a problem.

Access   Take the A39 into Porlock, then from here
the B3225 down to the break. Parking is available
above the break. There are two minor roads off the
A39 to Porlock Weir if you're coming from
Lynmouth, but there's a toll payable on both.

Facilities   Pub in village, and more facilities up the
hill in Porlock.

Accommodation   There are caravan parks and
camp sites at Porlock.

Opposite: Ruler-edge lines roll in to Lynmouth

SOUTH COAST

1 BOVISAND BAY, PLYMOUTH SOUND
➤ *Landranger 201, GR 506492*

Surf A right hand reef break that requires a big SW swell to work. It works from mid to low tide, and is best in a NW wind. Not recommended for beginners.

Access Take the A379 E out of Plymouth, and turn off at signs to Staddiscombe and/or Down Thomas. The bay can be reached from either village.

Facilities None.

Accomodation See Wembury.

2 WEMBURY BAY
➤ *Landranger 201, GR 516485*

Surf If Wembury is working you can be sure that there'll be plenty of people in the water. It's only

seven miles from Plymouth and well situated for surfers from the city. There are three breaks at Wembury.

Wembury Bay - This is the main break; it's mainly a left hander breaking off Blackstone Rocks over a rock and sand reef. It can hold waves well overhead in size. On a big swell it will work at all stages of the tide, but if the surf is small it's best from mid to low tide. It's offshore in winds from NW through to NE. OK for beginners.

Yealm sandbar - This is where to head for if you want to avoid the crowds. There's a fast, hollow, low tide right hander breaking over the sand bar that has developed in the estuary, but it requires a big S to SW swell to work. Not a beginners wave.

Gara Point - It's unlikely that you'll be surfing here unless you're a local because you need a boat to get to the break. It only works if conditions are ideal - a big S to SW swell with calm conditions or a gentle offshore wind - and it only starts breaking at around 8ft. It's rarely surfed, but if you do happen to get everything coming together at the right time and have the experience to surf big waves, you'll find a right hander jacking up out of deep water which can be good and hollow. Good luck!

Wembury is a protected area and a particularly attractive spot.

Access Take the minor road from the A379 at Plymstock to Wembury, from where a lane leads to the car park behind the beach.

Facilities Cafe and shop adjacent to beach. Toilets at car park.

Accommodation There's a caravan park and camp site at Brixton to the north, and at Newton Ferrers. There's a youth hostel in Plymouth.

3 MOTHECOMBE
➤ *Landranger 202, GR 615474*

Surf A beach break in the sheltered sandy estuary of the river Erme, with lefts and rights which work from low to mid tide. There are also waves at high tide breaking in a sheltered cove. It works on the swell pushed in by a SW gale and is protected from SW winds, but it needs a very big swell.

Access On the opposite side of the estuary from Wembury. Take the turn-off from the A379 just E of Yealmpton for Holbeton and Mothecombe. There's a car park about a quarter of a mile from the beach.

Facilities Shops, pub at Holbeton.

Accommodation See Wembury.

4 CHALLABOROUGH
➤ *Landranger 202, GR 648448*

Surf A beach break, mainly left handers, from low to mid tide. It needs a bigger swell than nearby Bantham, and is always smaller. It's offshore in NE winds, but will also work in NW winds. Can jack-up quickly to produce a very fast, heavy wave.

Access Take the B3392 to Bigbury off the A379, and turn off at Bigbury for Challaborough. There's a car park at the beach.

Facilities Shop at holiday camp behind beach.

Accommodation There's a youth hostel at Bigbury and the holiday camp.

5 BANTHAM
➤ *Landranger 202, GR 660440*

Surf The most consistent beach break in South Devon. A rivermouth break at the mouth of the river Avon in a very picturesque setting. It faces SW so picks up more swell than other south coast beaches.

There's a right hander at low to mid tide, which can be hollow, and a left and right-hand peak on the left of the beach at low to mid tide. It can hold waves up to about 8ft, then it tends to close out. You can get some long rides here - up to 200-300 yards on a good swell. Unlike most south coast beaches it's not too unusual to get waves here in the summer. E to NE winds are offshore.

This is a very popular break with Plymouth-based surfers, so don't be surprised to find crowds here when there's a good swell running. A good beginners wave, but you should watch out for a rip on the east side of the beach - this can get very strong when an outgoing tide combines with a heavy flow from the river.

Access From Plymouth and the south it's quickest to take the B3392 to Bigbury on Sea from the A379, which is on the opposite side of the estuary to Bantham, and park above the beach. You can easily paddle to the break from here. From the east and north take the signposted minor road to Bantham from the roundabout on the A379 at the junction with the B3197. There's a car park in the dunes above the beach.

Facilities There are shops and pubs in the nearby villages on both sides of the river. The beach is patrolled by lifeguards.

Accommodation There's a caravan park and camp site just outside Bantham, and plenty more around Salcombe, a few miles to the SE. There's a youth hostel in Bigbury and some rather expensive-looking hotels in the area.

6 THURLESTONE REEF
➤ *Landranger 202, 666425*

Surf A right hand reef break approximately a quarter of a mile out to sea in front of the golf course. It can hold very big waves, well over head high, but needs a big SW swell. Best on high tide. There are lots of rocks to watch out for. N to NE winds are offshore. Definitely a wave for experienced surfers only.

Access   From the B3197, which acts as a link road between the A379 and the A381, take the signposted turn-off SW to Thurlestone. Park above the beach.

Facilities   Limited facilities available in Thurlestone. Nearest big towns are Salcombe and Kingsbridge.

Accommodation   Plenty of caravan parks and camp sites around Salcombe. Youth hostel.

7 HOPE COVE
➤ Landranger 202, GR 675398

Surf   This is a relatively unknown spot which can produce a really good, hollow right hander on a big SW swell, breaking over a rock and sand bottom. It's very fickle however. It holds up to around 8ft after which it closes out. It's best two hours before high tide. This is a break for experienced surfers only because you take off in front of rocks and are then faced by a very hollow, tubing section. E winds are offshore.

Access   Take the signposted minor road west off the main A381 Salcombe road. You can park above the break.
Facilities   Limited facilities available in the village, otherwise head for Salcombe.

Accommodation   Caravan park, camp sites and hotels in and around nearby Salcombe. Youth hostel.

8 BOLT HEAD
➤ Landranger 202, GR 728361

Surf   A mid to high tide right hander breaking over a sandbar. It needs a big SW swell. There's a very bad rip at low tide. Best in calm conditions or with gentle winds from the north. Not a beginners wave.

Access   Drive S through Salcombe until the road ends. It's a long walk from here to the break.

Facilities   Cafes, shops, and pubs in abundance in Salcombe, but nothing near the headland.

Accommodation   See Hope Cove.

9 SALCOMBE
➤ Landranger 202, GR 731383

Surf   Surf can be found in the small SE facing cove

inside the river mouth. It's well sheltered from SW gales, and is a good place to head for when everywhere else is too big. It can give a beach break and works at all stages of the tide, although it tends to be best from low to mid tide. Generally OK for beginners, but watch out for rocks on the beach.

Access   The beach is on the S side of Salcombe, and there's car parking above it. However, Salcombe, being a very attractive old harbour and a boating centre, is very crowded at all times of the year and the traffic in the town is often very heavy.

Facilities and Accommodation   See Hope Cove and Bolt Head.

10 TORBAY AREA

Surf   There are a number of breaks in this area that will work when an easterly gale has been blowing. The beaches face east, so are directly in line to pick up any swell generated by such winds. While the winds are still blowing, conditions are going to be far from perfect. If you're lucky, the wind may veer round to the SW to give offshore conditions while the swell continues to come through. These conditions are only likely to persist for a short time.

GOODRINGTON SANDS: (Landranger 192, GR 894595) - Beach break with lefts and rights, but usually small and lacking in power.

PAIGNTON PIER: (GR 896609) - The pier picks up the most swell, with left and right-hand beach breaks to either side of it. It works from about 2ft to just overhead - as is generally the case with all the Torbay breaks.

THE GASWORKS: - A smooth rock reef break with lefts and rights.

LIVERMEAD: (GR 905627) - A variety of peaks, both lefts and rights, working from low to mid tide. No good at high tide because of the backwash off the sea wall.

TORRE ABBEY BAY: (GR 910636) - Only has a wave when everywhere else is too big, with a left breaking off the promenade wall. There's also a reef in the middle of the bay, but this is very rarely surfed.
    All these breaks are OK for beginners. Local surfers complain of sewage in the line up.

Access   The A379 runs along this stretch of coast,

with roads off to the various beaches. There are car parks above all the breaks.

Facilities   An ample supply of shops, cafes, and pubs near to all beaches. Lifeguards patrol the beaches in summer.

Accommodation   There are plenty of caravan parks and camp sites in the area and numerous hotels.

11 TEIGNMOUTH
➤ *Landranger 192, GR 945730*

Surf   A beach break with lefts and right, needs a big swell to work, but can also pick up those rare E'ly swells. Best from mid to high tide. NW winds are offshore, SW cross-shore. OK for beginners.

Access   The A381 runs directly into Teignmouth. Follow signs to the beach, where there are car parking facilities.

Facilities   Shops, cafe, and pubs in the town. Water skiing on the river.

Accommodation   There are plenty of caravan parks, camp sites and hotels in the area.

12 DAWLISH WARREN
➤ *Landranger 192, GR 985790*

Surf   Dawlish Warren is a fine example of over developement. One of its few saving graces is that it can occasionally - usually in winter - produce a wave. It's a beach break, with lefts and rights, working after strong S or E winds have been blowing, or on a huge SW swell. I received divided opinion on when it's best - some said low tide, others high tide. NW to N winds are offshore. OK for beginners.

Access   Signposted from the A379. Car parks above the beach at SW end. Also a train station above the beach at the SW end.

Facilities   In summer it has everything you could possibly need (other than a surf shop) from bucket and spade to video games and burgers and chips. In winter there's very little, although there's a pub just before the entrance to the beach. Lifeguards patrol the beach in summer.

Accommodation   Caravan parks and camp sites. Youth hostel in Exeter.

13 EXMOUTH
➤ *Landranger 192, GR 030798*

Surf   A south-facing beach which picks up big S and SW swells, but is generally a gutless wave. There are lefts and rights, best at high tide. Winds from the N are offshore. OK for beginners.

Access   The A376 from the north (which joins the M5 at nearby Exeter) goes straight into Exmouth. There's parking above the beach.

Facilities   Shops, cafes, pubs, etc. in Exmouth. Lifeguards in summer. (Also see Dawlish Warren).

Accomodation   Caravan park above the beach, also other camp sites locally. Youth hostel in Exeter.

14 SIDMOUTH
➤ *Landranger 192, GR 128872*

Surf   As with Exmouth, and other stretches of the coastline between Exmouth and Lyme Regis to the NW, the waves here rarely have much power, and require very big swells to produce any surf at all. When it's working, a beach break, lefts and rights; best at high tide. NW winds offshore. OK for beginners.

Access   From the A3052 take the B3175 which goes straight into Sidmouth. Park where you can, walk down steps from promenade to beach.
Facilities   Shops, cafes, and pubs in the town. Sailboard hire available. The beach is patrolled at weekends by the Seaton Inshore Rescue Club. Seaton is a pleasant spot to visit even if there is no surf, being a well-preserved Regency resort which has not become over-commercialised and has managed to retain its quiet charm.

Accommodation   There are caravan parks and camp sites out towards Salcombe Regis.

5 THE SOUTH COAST OF ENGLAND & THE ISLE OF WIGHT

This section covers a relatively large area, from Dorset in the west through Hampshire, West and East Sussex, to Kent in the east. And then there's the Isle of Wight.

It has to be said that it's not an area that one readily associates with surfing, and apart from the odd exception such as Kimmeridge, it's not a stretch of coastline that you'd go out of your way to reach

for surf. Swells here are rare outside the winter months, and result from either very localised weather systems giving short lived swells from local winds, or big Atlantic swells pushing up the Channel from, ideally, a deep low in the Bay of Biscay (East Kent, on the other hand can pick up North Sea swells).

Any clean groundswells making their way up the Channel find it difficult to persist because the

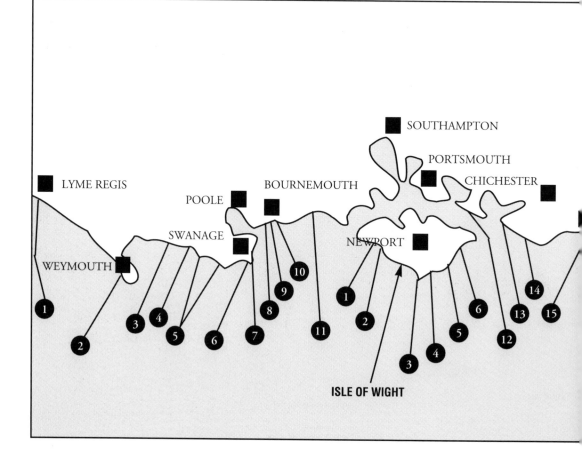

narrowing of the Channel increases the strength of the tidal streams, and the further east you go the more this will tend to weaken the swell.

You may get wind-blown surf from SW gales as a low pressure system moves in from the Atlantic. So onshore waves are what you're most likely to find yourself surfing on the south coast, as they're far more common than clean surf and offshore winds. Few places other than Kimmeridge can be expected to get waves over head high.

Having gone to such lengths to decry the area, however, let me say that good waves can still be had if you're in the right place at the right time. On a big swell Kimmeridge can produce a reef break to rival most and west of here towards Weymouth are a number of good breaks; some very isolated and still awaiting discovery.

On the whole, the South Coast is very much an 'urban' surf zone - most of the beaches are in, or close to, major towns and harbours. This has led to two things, neither of which are particularly popular in the surfing world - crowds and pollution. The pollution comes in many forms - marine litter from the busy shipping lanes in the Channel, sewage sludge dumped off the Thames estuary, and nuclear and industrial discharges at various points.

THE CLIMATE

Being at the southern end of the British Isles, the South Coast is one of the mildest parts of the country. But it can still get pretty cold in the winter. Average winter air temperatures are around 9°C (46 °F), but this may drop dramatically if easterly winds are blowing in from the Continent. The water temperature can get as low as 4-8°C (36-44°F).

If you're lucky enough to get surf in summer, you'll find air temperatures averaging 21°C (70°F), although it can get considerably warmer. The sea may get as warm as 18°C (66°F).

At most breaks, winds from a northerly quarter are offshore, which, particularly in winter, means perfect conditions are almost bound to be cold. In

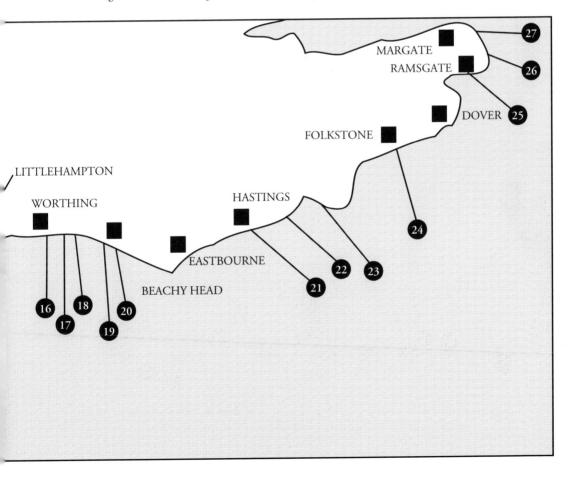

winter you'll need a 5mm steamer, gloves, boots and hood. In summer a 3mm steamer or maybe even a spring suit will suffice.

1 LYME REGIS, THE HARBOUR WALL
➤ *Landranger 193, GR 338915*

Surf   The harbour (The Cobb) wall is famed more for having been stood upon by Meryl Streep during filming of The French Lieutenant's Woman than for its surf. However, on a very big SW swell there's a left and right here from low to mid tide. It's at it's best in a NW wind. This is not a beginners wave.

Access   The A3052 and A3070 run straight into Lyme Regis. There's a car park by the pier.

Facilities   Shops, cafes, pubs, etc. in the town. The coastline east towards Golden Cap is well worth a visit if the surf's flat.

Accommodation   Caravan parks and camp sites at Uplyme and Charmouth.

2 FORTUNESWELL - WEST BAY
➤ *Landranger 194, GR 684733*

Surf   On a big, clean Channel groundswell there's a right hander off rocks at the SE end of the huge shingle bank that is Chesil beach. It works from mid to high tide and is best in NW to NE winds. Not a beginners wave.

Access   The A354 from Portland runs S into Fortuneswell. Park above the beach.
Facilities   Refreshments available in Fortuneswell.

Accommodation   Not a great deal of choice locally, your best bet is probably to head back towards Weymouth.

3 MUPE BAY
➤ *Landranger 194, GR 845799*

Surf   This is an isolated, rarely surfed reef break, requiring a good-sized SW swell to work. You really have to be into exploring or solitude to want to surf here.

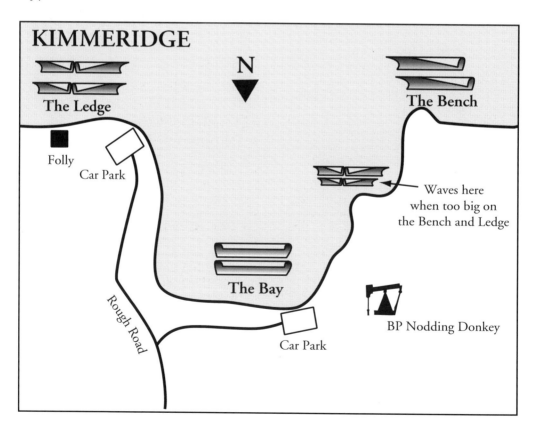

Access It's a two-mile walk east from Lulworth along the cliff top.

Facilities None.

Accommodation Caravan site and youth hostel at West Lulworth.

4 KIMMERIDGE
► *Landranger 195, GR 900790*

Surf (see diagram) This is the jewel in the crown of South Coast surfing. Kimmeridge can produce excellent waves, and can also hold a big swell - 12 feet plus has been surfed here.
   Kimmeridge picks up more swell than anywhere else in the area because the swell is enhanced by Kimmeridge Ledge, a rocky shelf which is between one and four fathoms below the surface and extends for five miles from Gad Cliff in the west to St Albans Head in the east. There are four breaks at Kimmeridge.
   BROAD BENCH - Picks up any swell going, and on a SW swell will be the biggest place in the area. It's a right hander, breaking over a flat rock shelf, which works at all stages of the tide. It can get BIG here, and is a long way out from the shore, with a long paddle out from the bay. Not a wave for inexperienced surfers. Also a very hollow, short left, breaks here. Both waves break in shallow water.
   Inside the Bench there's a right-hander which works when the Bench, or the Ledge on the other side of the bay, are too big.
   THE BAY - Slow rights and lefts over a flat rock shelf, which only works on a big swell. It's nowhere near the quality of the other breaks at Kimmeridge, and is only really worth surfing if they're too big and out of control.
   THE LEDGES - Another reef break over a flat rock shelf, with both rights and lefts, the lefts being better. It picks up most SW swells. Best a couple of hours either side of high tide. There's a rip on the right of the break which can take you back into the bay. You paddle out from beneath Clavell Tower, the folly on the clifftop. You will have to hop over rocks, so boots should be worn even in summer.
   Winds from NW to NE are best for all the breaks - SW (onshore) winds really mess it up. Kimmeridge is nearly always crowded when there's a good swell running.

Access This is a rather tortuous process. There's a narrow road to Kimmeridge off the A351 Wareham-Swanage road, and you have to pay to get down to the beach - along a pretty rough road - as the bay is

privately owned. There's car parking in front of the bay, or out towards The Ledge. Resticted access to Broad Bench, as it's in a Army firing range.

Facilities Auxiliary coastguards patrol the beach at weekends and during rough weather in summer. Ice cream kiosk and toilets near the beach.

Accommodation Camp site about three miles away at Church Knowle, otherwise very little locally. There is a youth hostel in Swanage.

5 ROPE LAKE HEAD AREA

Surf As with the coast to the W of Kimmeridge, this is a somewhat isolated and infrequently surfed area suited to those surfers who like to explore. It's well exposed to the same swells that get into Kimmeridge, being on the W side of St Alban's Head. There are both reef and beach breaks to be found, although the information I was able to obtain was pretty sketchy - hence the lack of details. Winds from N are offshore. This is an area for experienced surfers only, and the locals are very protective of 'their' waves.

Access There are no roads along this stretch of coast - and you'll need a good map to find your way there.

Facilities None.

Accommodation See Kimmeridge.

6 DURLSTON HEAD
► *Landranger 195, GR 035773*

Surf This is a right-hand point break which only works on a huge SW swell. It has the advantage of being sheltered by the headland from SW winds, whilst W winds are offshore. It can be pretty hollow at low tide, but is not really surfable at high tide due to backwash off the cliffs. You have to paddle out over rocks, which can make getting back in tricky. You should also watch out for tidal races around the headland. This is definitely a break for experienced surfers only.

Access Drive S from Swanage to the Head and Durlston Country Park. Park at the headland, from where there's a tricky descent down the cliffs to the break.

Facilities None.

Accommodation   Caravan park and camp sites. Youth hostel.

7 SWANAGE
➤ Landranger 195, GR 030790

Surf   Swanage has surf only on the biggest of swells - Bournemouth has to be overhead before it starts to work here. There are right and left hand beach breaks. Best from low tide towards high water. W winds are offshore. OK for beginners. Swanage is one of Britain's few 'Blue Flag' beaches.

Access   The A351 takes you into the town; you can park on the sea front. Traffic can be a problem in summer, but it's highly unlikely you'd find surf here then.

Facilities   Everything you'd expect of a small, popular seaside resort, including diving, sailing, and fishing - although if the weather is such that you're checking Swanage for surf you'd hardly be likely to be doing any of these recreations as an alternative.

Accommodation   See Durlston Head.

8 BOURNEMOUTH PIER
➤ Landranger 195, GR 089907

Surf   If you don't like crowds, steer clear of Bournemouth. The pier will get waves from both SW and E swells.It also produces a surfable wave in a SW gale, when the left side of the pier tends to be better as it's sheltered somewhat from the wind. The left side has a right, the right side has a left - usually shorter, and it only really works well on an E swell. Bournemouth Pier will hold waves up to about head-high. On a big swell there'll be surf at all stages of the tide. On a small swell it's better on the push from low tide up. Winds from N are offshore. Bad rips on SE winds.

This is an OK spot for beginners, but remember to observe the drop-in rule and don't get in the way of others - there'll be lots of them! If the crowds are just too much for you at the Bournemouth Pier, you may find similar quality surf to the SW at Branksome, Canford Cliffs, or Sandbanks.

Access   All roads on this stretch of the coast lead to Bournemouth, and there are good road and motorway links with London. There's plenty of parking close to the beach, although it may not be easy to find a space in summer or at weekends.

Facilities   Being a major holiday resort, Bournemouth has just about everything, even closed circuit television so that 'Big Brother' can keep an eye on beach users.

The nightlife in Bournemouth is pretty good and can be extremely entertaining - but I don't have the time or space to go into more details here!

Surf reports for the area can be obtained on Power FM (103.2 MHz) at around 9.30 am.

See Appendix for local surf shops.

Accommodation   Caravan parks and camp sites are few and far between in the immediate area, but there are plenty between Poole and Wareham.

9 BOSCOMBE PIER
➤ Landranger 195, GR 112912

Surf   There are waves both sides of the pier, with a right hander off the left (W) side, and a left off the right (E) side. It picks up waves from both SW and E swells, and also works in SW winds, but not as well as Bournemouth. The waves will vary depending on the quality of the sandbanks, which shift around a lot. On a big swell there'll be waves right through the tides, on a small swell it's better on the push. N to NE winds are offshore. OK for beginners - but don't get wrapped around the pier.

Access   Boscombe is just E of Bournemouth on the A35, with a signposted road down to the pier, or you can make your way along the coast from Bournemouth pier. There's parking above the beach.

Facilities   Shops, toilets, etc. above the beach and in the town - also see Bournemouth.
Accommodation   See Bournemouth. There are also caravan sites on the outskirts of nearby Christchurch.

10 SOUTHBOURNE
➤ Landranger 195, GR 143912

Surf   The beach faces SSW, and picks up big SW swells. It's a beach break, with both lefts and rights. As with most of the beaches in the vicinity it works all through the tide on a big swell, but is best on the push on a small swell. N to NE winds are offshore. OK for beginners.

Access   A couple of miles E of Boscombe, you can either get there along the coast, or on the B3059 turn-off from the A35. Park above the beach.

Facilities   Shops and toilets close to the beach. Christchurch harbour, just to the E, is a popular boardsailing and sailing area.

Accommodation   See Boscombe.

11 HIGHCLIFFE
➤ *Landranger 195, GR 204930*

Surf   On a very big swell there's a mixed reef/beach break here. Beach breaks can also be found along the coast at Barton-on-Sea and Milford-on-Sea, which face more SSW, so are in a better position to pick up SW swells. Once again, there'll be waves all through the tide on a big swell, while on small swells it's better on the push. N to NE winds are offshore. OK for beginners.

Access   The A337 runs through Highcliffe and Barton, with the B3058 branching off it into Milford. There's parking above the beach.

Facilities   Shop/cafe in grounds of Highcliffe Castle. Lifeguards in summer.

Acommodation   There are a number of caravan parks and camp sites inland.

12 SOUTH HAYLING, HAYLING ISLAND
➤ *Landranger 197*

Surf   Hayling is blocked off from swells to a large extent by the Isle of Wight, so it needs to be a big SW swell for waves to appear here - although it will also get waves from a good E swell. There are several breaks to be found along the five-mile long south-facing pebble beach. There's a reef break, a break off the sand bar, a break at the entrance to Chichester Harbour (watch out for currents here), and a common or garden beach break. The waves are best just before and after high tide. N winds are offshore.
   The beach is OK for beginners, but there are quite strong inshore currents to watch out for on a big swell.

Access   The A3203 branches off the A27 and goes straight to the coast. There is plenty of parking above the beach.

Facilities   There are several kiosks and cafes above

Board meeting!

the beach, and public toilets. Hayling is a major boardsailing venue.

Accommodation   Caravan parks and camp sites on the island.

13 WEST WITTERING
➤ *Landranger 197, GR 770980*

Surf   The Witterings coastline faces directly SW, so although SW swells are blocked to an extent by the Isle of Wight, it's still well situated to pick up more swell than anywhere else in the area. It's a popular spot with London-based surfers, but it's a long stretch of beach which can cope reasonably well with crowds. It's also very popular with board sailors. Things can get pretty hectic in the surf on days when there's a strong wind-blown swell and both surfers and board sailors take to the water.

West Wittering is a beach break close to the mouth of Chichester harbour, with lefts and rights that can be fast and hollow on a good clean swell. It's only really surfable around high tide, and on small tides (less than 4.0 metres), or big ones over about 5.0 metres, the waves are rarely very good. NE winds are offshore. It's not an ideal break for beginners, as there's often a fast drift around the mouth of the harbour - to the right on the flood and to the left on the ebb.

Access   The B2179 runs down towards the beach. There's a large car park, from where you walk to the break.

Facilities   Limited facilities in the car park - shops, cafes, pubs up the road at East Wittering.
Accommodation   Plenty of caravan parks and camp sites in the area.

14 EAST WITTERING
➤ *Landranger 197, GR 805964*

Surf   There are beach break peaks up and down the beach at East Wittering. There are waves right through from low to high tide, although it's usually better around high tide. East Wittering will hold a wave of sorts in a SW gale, but it's only surfable at high tide in these conditions, as there's a massive paddle out through line after line of white water as the tide drops. Having said it's best at high tide, you need to watch out for the groynes along the coast, and there's a surprisingly heavy shore-break.

There's also a wave 200 yards east of the main break, at the 'Barn', where an old wreck (marked by

a red buoy) can produce waves (mainly lefts) at low tide on a clean swell. Around mid tide there may also be a wave here as the tide moves over a sandbar near the red buoy.

NE winds are offshore. East Wittering is a popular spot with novices, but make sure you can cope with the crowds in the water on busy days.

Access   The B2198 (Shore Road) ends in front of the beach. There's often a parking space within walking distance of the beach.

Facilities   There are shops and cafes close to the beach. Particularly convenient is the Shore pub, a stone's throw from the beach and a popular spot with both surfers and board sailors. The Shore is always heaving at the weekend if there's surf or wind - or both - and it's a good place to meet the locals.

Accommodation   See West Wittering.

15 LITTLEHAMPTON, WEST BEACH
➤ *Landranger 197, GR 235044*

Surf   A S facing beach, with a wave at it's E end, where a large jetty protects a deep water entrance to Littlehampton marina. SW swells hit the end of the jetty, wedge up, and literally double in size to give a short right and a longer left over a sand bottom. It's best around high tide, and in winds from a N'ly quarter. OK for beginners, but take care not to get swept into the jetty. N'ly winds are offshore.

Access   Car park above beach.

Facilities   Refreshments available in the town.

Accommodation   There's a caravan site and a youth hostel inland near Warningcamp.

16 SOUTH LANCING, WEST BEACH
➤ *Landranger 198 GR 235044*

Surf   A beach break which works best two hours either side of high tide when the wind drops or goes offshore after a S'ly or S-W'ly gale. It's considerably less crowded than the more popular breaks at Brighton.

Access   Parking 500 yards east of Brooklands Pleasure Park on the A259.

Facilities   Shops, cafes and pubs in Lancing, plus the 'pleasure park'.

17 SHOREHAM-BY-SEA, HARBOUR WALL
➤ *Landranger 198, GR 234045*

Surf This is a left-hand beach break running down the harbour wall, which works in a heavy SW or W wind, Force 6 plus. It can hold waves from 3 to 6 feet in height. On a big swell it can give a long ride, but it gets crowded, and there's not a lot of room, so inexperienced surfers should bear this in mind. N winds are offshore. Best from mid to low tide.

Access From the car park at the end of the industrial road running along the seaward side of Shoreham harbour. This is reached from the A259 coast road. It's a long walk along the sea wall from the car park to the break.

Facilities None at the break.

Accommodation Little in the way of camp sites locally. There is a youth hostel in Brighton.

18 PORTSLADE, THE OLD POWER STATION
➤ *Landranger 198, GR 250047*

Surf A beach break working on big SW swells, best from mid tide up, producing typical south coast rollers. It's at it's best either side of high tide when the sea is below the end of the pebble beach and the concrete outfall is exposed. N winds are offshore. OK for beginners, but watch out for the breakwaters and jetty as the tide drops.

Access From the A259 at the windsurfing lake. The road runs along the seaward side of Shoreham harbour. Park at the end then walk back to the jetty opposite the old Shoreham power station site.

Facilities None.

Accommodation See Shoreham (above).

19 BRIGHTON, THE PIERS

Surf Famed for anything but it's surf, but a popular spot and crowds can be a problem. Along the shingle beach around the piers you may find a beach break on a big SW swell. It's best from mid to low tide, and back up to mid - it dumps on the shingle bank at high tide. N to NE winds are offshore. OK for beginners, but keep well clear of the piers.

Access The A259 runs along the seafront, with expensive parking all the way along.

Facilities The beach is patrolled by lifeguards from May to September. Food, drink and nightlife are all in abundant supply, especially in summer - unfortunately the same can't be said of the surf at that time of the year. On a more cultural level there's an art gallery and museum, and, of course, the Royal Pavillion.

Accommodation For a major holiday town, Brighton is surprisingly lacking in camp sites; the only one being above the marina on the E side of the town. There's a youth hostel to the north of the town.

20 BRIGHTON, BLACK ROCK, THE MARINA

Surf This is one of the more popular spots on this stretch of the S coast, and is a beach break over a chalk reef. As with all the breaks in SE England, it requires a big swell to work, when it may throw up lefts and rights from 3 to 5 feet in height - perhaps bigger in a heavy SW gale. N to NE winds are offshore. There are some minor hazards in the form of chalk and flint rocks on the sea floor. Beware of gullies on a dropping tide, and a W to E drift. OK for beginners. Water pollution can be a problem in this area.

Access The marina is alongside the A259 coast road, with parking available on the cliff top by the golf course.

Facilities Refreshment locally and in Brighton.

Accommodation See Brighton.

21 HASTINGS PIER
➤ *Landranger 199, GR 812090*

Surf A pebbly beach break which requires a big SW swell, usually pushed in by a gale from the same direction and at the same time. Winds from the SW should be in excess of Force 4 at least. It's best on a dropping tide, although it works either side of high water. At high tide the waves are heavy close outs, and at low tide they tend to back off. NW winds are offshore. Fine for beginners as long as you keep clear of the pier.

60

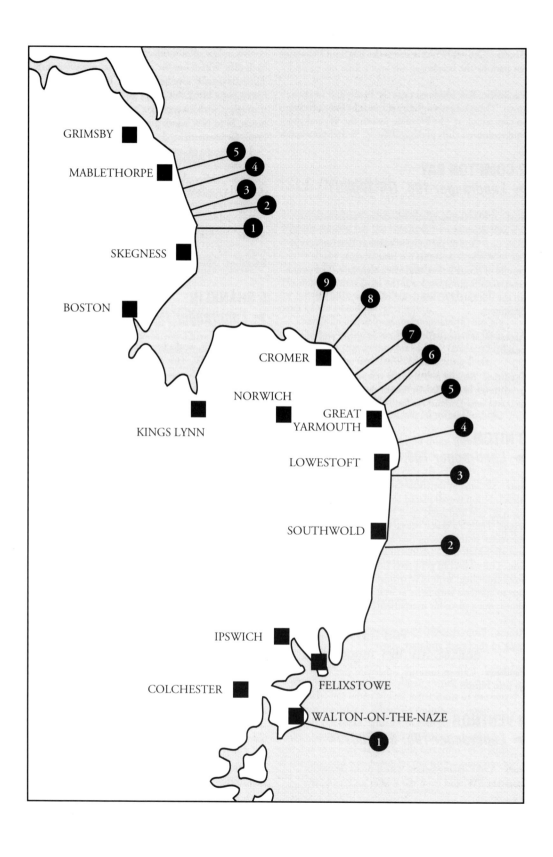

6 EAST ANGLIA & LINCOLNSHIRE

This part of England is famed for its flat countryside - unfortunately the surf is often much the same, and it's not an area that is likely to attract too many travelling surfers. However, it can have reasonable waves at times, particularly in winter, and it may be worth a visit to one of the breaks if you happen to be in the area and have a board with you.

The best surf is generally to be found in winter, when severe storms to the north send groundswells down the North Sea that are powerful enough to make their way over the shallow sea floor and into the beaches. Waves can be found at other times of the year too, but far less frequently. A deep depression over SE England or the Low Countries may also creat a short-lived S-SE swell.

Crystal clear water is a rarity here, although it's not necessarily pollution that's to blame. The shallow sea floor is easily disturbed by swells and currents, which stir up sediment and hold it in murky suspension. With this almost constant shifting around of the sea bed, sand banks that produce a break are usually only temporary features, and the quality of the breaks on most beaches will change frequently.

Pollution can be a problem in this part of the North Sea. Everything from sewage to radioactive and industrial waste is pumped or dumped into the sea, having a harmful effect on most of its marine life, which must include surfers.

CLIMATE

Being shallow, the North Sea warms quickly in summer and may reach around 18°C (64°F). For the same reason, it cools very quickly in the winter when the water soon becomes very cold indeed and the temperature may fall as low as 4°C (39°F).

In summer, this part of England can be one of the warmest places in the British Isles; but in winter, especially in calm anti-cyclonic conditions, it can be one of the coldest. When the surf is at it's best, you can generally expect the water temperature, and possibly the air temperature, to be at their lowest.

1 WALTON-ON-THE-NAZE, ESSEX
► *Landranger 169, GR 255215*

Surf This is one of the nearest breaks to London, but it works very infrequently. If a NE gale has been blowing for a few days you may find a small wave by the pier - the second longest in Britain (the pier, not the wave). It's best from half tide towards high water. NW winds are offshore, but the swell won't hang around for long once the winds that produced it die away. OK for beginners.

Access The B1336 and B1034 run into the town and close by the pier. Parking available within easy reach of the beach.

Facilities Plenty of refreshment facilities along the promenade and in the town. Lifeguards in summer.

Accommodation Caravan parks and camp sites are few and far between and mostly to be found near Clacton.

2 WALBERSWICK, SUFFOLK
► *Landranger 156, GR 500745*

Surf Another spot that only works infrequently. On very low tides there's a break over a sandbar some 50m offshore. It works after a SW or NW gale, with a right on a SW swell and a left on a NW swell. NW to W winds are offshore. OK for beginners.

Access The B1387 branches off the A12 and runs straight into Walberswick. There's free parking just above the beach.

Facilities Refreshments available in the town.

Accommodation Not a great deal locally.

3 LOWESTOFT, SUFFOLK
► *Landranger 134, GR 545519*

Surf A swell from either N or S may produce reasonable waves at Lowestoft, particularly by

Claremont pier on South Beach. SW gales can also produce swells that wrap into the beach, with a SW wind being offshore. Winds through from SW to N are offshore to cross shore to varying degrees; so Lowestoft can also be worth checking if the N-facing beaches around Runton and Cromer are blown out. Best around low tide, although it can be surfed at all stages. Beware of the pier and the numerous groynes. OK for beginners.

Access   The A12 runs above the beach; there are plenty of parking places. Surfers arriving by train will be pleased to note that the beach is a short walk from the train station.

Facilities   Lowestoft is a popular holiday town as well as a fishing port, and has no shortage of cafes, shops, pubs, etc. See appendix for details of local surf shops.

Accommodation   Plenty of caravan parks and camp sites in the area.

4 GORLESTON, NORFOLK
➤ *Landranger 134, GR 530030*

Surf   The Norfolk coastline presents one unbroken strip of alternating sand and pebble beaches from the mouth of the river Yare all the way up to Sheringham. The sand banks upon which the waves break can change shape and position, and, in bad storms, even disappear overnight. The quality of the waves will vary all the time. The beaches are covered with millions of pieces of flint from shallow chalk reefs offshore. On a good swell there will be waves most of the way along the coast: the breaks described here are those which are easiest to reach or the best known.
Gorleston can get a left off the harbour wall, which provides some protection from blustery winds. There are also beach breaks to the south.
It's offshore in a NW to W wind. OK for beginners.

Access   A turn-off from the A12 goes into Gorleston. Park by the beach.

Facilities   Refreshments etc. available above the beach and in the town. Lifeguard in summer.

Accommodation   See Great Yarmouth.

5 GREAT YARMOUTH, NORFOLK

Surf   Not a particularly good wave but Great Yarmouth is bigger on a N swell than Lowestoft. It works when an E gale has been blowing for a couple of days, and when a SW gale is blowing and holding up the waves. It tends to be better from low to mid tide, on a rising tide. There are waves all along the beach; the quality - or lack of it - depending upon the state of the banks. Occasionally you may find waves off the two piers and the jetty, especially Britannia Pier. There can be strong N or S longshore drifts on larger swells. W winds are offshore. OK for beginners.

Access   The A47 from inland, and the A12 from the south, run into the town, from where you follow signs to the beach. There are various car parks all along the seafront.

Facilities   Great Yarmouth is a pretty large holiday resort, so there are all the facilities you're likely to need along the beach. Lifeguards patrol the beach in summer.

Accommodation   There are numerous caravan parks and camp sites and a youth hostel.

6 CAISTER-ON-SEA TO HEMSBY HOLE, NORFOLK

Surf   There are waves to be found all along this stretch of coast, which gradually curves around from the S to face NNE. The waves will be better on a N swell, breaking over sand bars, with the lefts tending to be best. SW to W winds are offshore. OK for beginners. This is the nearest you'll get in Britain to surfing in California (check a detailed map for further information!).

Access   There's access to the beach at various points along this stretch of coast, on minor roads from the A149 and B1159. Parking can be difficult at some places in summer, but no problem in winter.

Facilities   In summer there should be some refreshments close to most breaks, in winter you're more likely to have to go into the nearest town.

Accommodation   Caravan parks and camp sites all along the coast. Alternative accommodation in Great Yarmouth.

7 WALCOTT, NORFOLK
➤ *Landranger 133, GR 360330*

Surf Walcott is just one surf spot along Norfolk's NE-facing stretch of coastline, and you may find waves at any of the various points of access to the beach N and S of here. If the waves further south are too small on a N'ly swell, they'll be bigger here. Walcott has waves breaking over a sand bar, which are often bigger than they look from the sea wall. It's better at low tide, when you must paddle over a channel to get out to the break. It can be difficult getting across the channel on an incoming tide. SW winds are offshore. OK for beginners.

Access Turn off the B1159 to the beach and park by the sea wall.

Facilities Refreshments available in the town.

Accommodation Caravan site at Bacton (which may also have a wave). See Cromer.

8 CROMER, NORFOLK
➤ *Landranger 133, GR 220425*

Surf The coast around Cromer faces NE to NNE, and is exposed to N groundswells coming down the North Sea. Because of this, it tends to be both more consistent and more popular than the beaches further S. Cromer has a beach break over a sand and pebble bottom, usually working at most stages of the tide. It can be good on the E side of the pier around low tide. However, there's heavy pollution here from raw sewage. There's a longshore drift from W to E on an incoming tide, and vice-versa on the ebb. OK for beginners.

Access All the main roads are well signposted for Cromer. There's limited parking along the sea front.

Facilities Cafes and shops close to the beach and in the town.

Accommodation There are plenty of caravan parks and camp sites in the area and a youth hostel in Sheringham.

9 EAST RUNTON, NORFOLK
➤ *Landranger 133, GR 201429*

Surf The most popular break in East Anglia. It's a beach break, which only works from mid tide to high water. There's a flint and chalk reef just offshore which blocks the swell below mid tide. The best waves tend to be to the N of the sewer pipe (of which more later), with both lefts and rights. This can shift to the S of the pipe as the tide ebbs.

Under ideal conditions - NW groundswell and light offshore wind - Runton can very occasionally hold overhead, hollow waves. The break is very exposed, and blown out easily if the wind is in the wrong direction. Offshore winds are from the S to SW.

There are three hazards to be taken into account at Runton. The first is the shingle and flint to be found littering the gulley scoured out by the sea towards the bottom of the beach - this can cause cuts and bruises if you are dumped by the shore break. Next, there's the longshore current, which carries you SE on a rising tide, NW on an ebb tide. And finally, there's the sewer pipe: it's easy to surf into it or wipe out on it. Other than this, it's fine for beginners!

Access The A149 from Cromer to Sheringham runs parallel with the beach, with parking by the beach and a path down the low cliffs to the beach.

Facilities Limited refreshment facilities in summer, which are likely to become non-existent in winter. If this is the case head into Cromer or Sheringham.

Accommodation See Cromer.

Breaks similar to those at Cromer and Runton can also be found at Overstrand (faces NE), three miles E of Cromer, Sheringham (faces N), just W of Runton, and Cley-next-the-Sea (N facing), five miles W of Sheringham. The longshore drift tends to become stronger the further west you go. The tidal stream runs from E to W on the ebb, and from W to E on the flood. These breaks are not likely to be any better than those at Cromer and Runton, but are an alternative if Cromer and Runton are crowded.

LINCOLNSHIRE

Without wishing to sound churlish, Lincolnshire really has to be considered as something of a last resort as far as surfing is concerned. There are waves here, but they very rarely have any quality, and never exceed head height.

The Lincolnshire coastline consists, more or less, of one long, flat, sandy beach facing NNE. This slopes very gently and produces slow and gutless waves. The peaks shift constantly, breaking over ever-moving sandbanks. The sand itself overlies brown mud and clay, which is often disturbed by the breaking waves to give the water a very murky look. The suspended clay and silt often manages to transfer itself to your board and wetsuit. Chris Reed, a surfer who has had a fair amount of experience of Lincolnshire waves, described it to me: "You'll end up with a brown suit, brown face, brown board, and browned off!" Another thing to bear in mind is that there are groynes all along the coast which must be avoided when surfing.

For those who still wish to surf here after such a flattering description of the place, I've listed below a number of spots which may have surf on a good swell. What you should look for is a big groundswell coming down from the north, or a swell developing from a couple of days or so of easterly gales. I haven't gone into much detail on each individual break, as they're all pretty much the same, being shifting beach breaks, generally at their best just before and just after high tide.

All can be reached quite easily from the A52, and there are a few caravan parks and camp sites in the area.

1 CHAPEL ST LEONARDS
➤ *Landranger 122, GR 564722*

Can't be surfed at high tide because of proximity of sea defences and groynes. Parking above beach, refreshments in town.

2 HUTTOFT BEACH
➤ *Landranger 122, GR 542787*

Park above beach at S end of Sandilands golf course. No facilities.

3 SANDILANDS
➤ *Landranger 122, GR 535797*

Park in golf club car park, or by slipway to beach. Refreshments available in village.

4 SUTTON ON SEA
➤ *Landranger 122, GR 525814*

The most popular surf spot in Lincolnshire. Easy access. Park on Church Lane at S end of town by the slipway. Plenty of shops, etc. in town.

5 MABLETHORPE

Park by slipway at end of the main street through town. Plenty of facilities here as Mablethorpe is a popular holiday town.

Although experienced surfers clearly wouldn't go a bundle on Lincolnshire surf, it's a good place for beginners, and seems to be particularly popular with youngsters on boogie boards.

Opposite: A taste of things to come in the North East of England

70

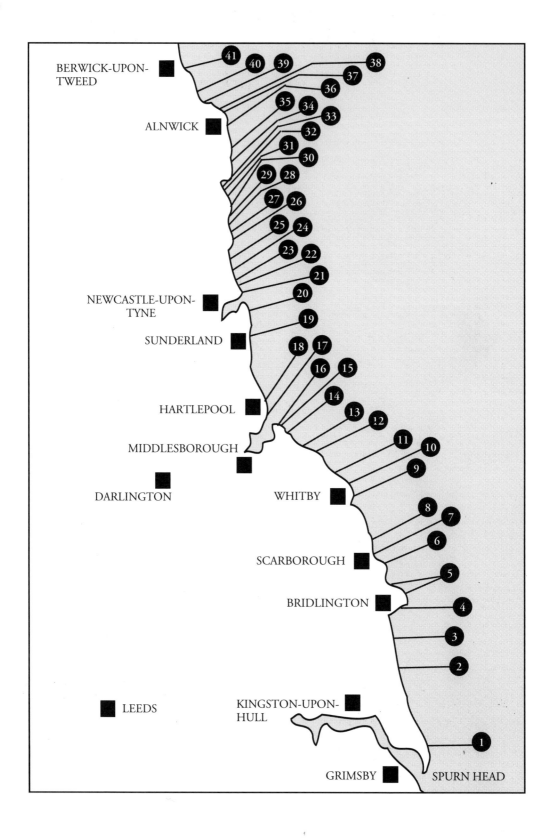

BERWICK-UPON-TWEED

ALNWICK

NEWCASTLE-UPON-TYNE

SUNDERLAND

HARTLEPOOL

MIDDLESBOROUGH

DARLINGTON

WHITBY

SCARBOROUGH

BRIDLINGTON

LEEDS

KINGSTON-UPON-HULL

GRIMSBY

SPURN HEAD

7 NORTH EAST ENGLAND

This stretch of coastline, from the Scottish border in the north to the Yorkshire coast in the south, is probably the most under-rated in Britain. It has an excellent selection of beach and reef breaks, some of which can throw up clean, powerful waves in both summer and winter. Prevailing winds are offshore.

The quality of the waves in this area has only recently begun to be recognised, and the number of surfers here is growing annually.

THE CLIMATE

Unfortunately, although the surf in NE England can be unexpectedly good, for every plus there has to be a minus, and the area has a big one - the cold.

As with Scotland, both the air and water temperature can be almost unbearable at times in winter unless you're a local or give yourself time to acclimatize. You'll need the best winter steamer you can get, and boots, gloves, and hood are an absolute necessity. Even so, in the depths of winter, the iron grip of the icy North Sea will still get to you after an hour or so. Water temperatures average 5-9°C (38-46°F) and air temperatures average 7°C (42°F), but both can get considerably lower.

Fortunately, there is still good quality surf available in the summer, and then the temperature is not too bad. Air temperatures will be between 18°C - 25°C (65°-77°F), whilst water temperature may reach around 15°C (58°F). The best surf results from deep lows over Scandinavia or the NE Atlantic, although lows over Denmark and the Low Countries can also produce good surf. These conditions are often completely independent of weather conditions in the UK, so as the prevailing winds are SW it's more common to get a combination of offshore winds and surf here than on the west coast of Britain.

1 WITHERNSEA - HUMBERSIDE
➤ Landranger 107 GR 344280

Surf A beach break, with lefts and rights, up to about head-high. The peaks tend to shift around due to a moving sand bottom. Withernsea is best on a N swell, but swells here can drop off very quickly. There are groynes all along the beach. It's generally better at low tide, partly because the tide is below the groynes then. There is a strong longshore current on a good-size swell, so constant paddling is necessary if you don't want to drift down to Spurn Head. SW winds are directly offshore. OK if you're a beginner, but you must look out for the groynes and be able to cope with the current.

There are similar quality waves to the S of Withernsea, around Nevill's Farm. As you have to pass through the farm to get to the beach make sure you're not trespassing before you do so.

Although not as good or consistent as the beaches to the north, Withernsea and the surrounding area provide the nearest waves for surfers based in Hull, South Yorkshire and the the north Midlands.

Access Withernsea is at the end of the A1033 from Hull, the B1362, and the B1242 coast road from the N. There's parking above the beach.

Facilities Shops, cafes, and pubs above the beach in the town.

Accommodation There are several caravan parks and camp sites along the coast.

2 HORNSEA - HUMBERSIDE
➤ Landranger 107 GR 210480

Surf A beach break, with lefts and rights, similar to Withernsea. Better at low tide, and on a N swell. There are longshore currents, but they are not as bad as those at Withernsea. SW winds are offshore. OK for beginners, but watch out for the currents.

There are breaks up and down the coast both N and S of Hornsea; all pretty similar to those you'll find here. The longshore current tends to become weaker as you move further N.

Access The B1242 coast road runs through Hornsea, and the B1244 runs into the town from inland. Parking above the beach.

Facilities Hornsea is a popular seaside town, so it's

busy in summer. There are cafes and amusement arcades within easy reach of the beach. Lifeguards patrol the beach on summer weekends.
Accommodation Numerous caravan parks and camp sites within easy reach.

3 FRAISTHORPE - HUMBERSIDE
➤ *Landranger 101 GR 170620*

Surf A beach break, directly in front of the caravan park. It continues N to join Bridlington South Sands, with peaks all the way along. Best at low tide. Similar in many respects to the beaches around Withernsea and Hornsea, except that it faces ESE, so picks up more S and E swell. OK for beginners, although there's a longshore current to watch out for as the swell picks up. W to WNW winds are offshore.

Access The A165 Hull-Bridlington road runs through the village. Turn east to the coast and the caravan park.

Facilities Limited facilities, but the large resort of

Bridlington is only five miles up the coast.

Accommodation Caravan park above the beach, and plenty more caravan parks and camp sites in the area. There are several cheap hotels in and around Bridlington.

4 BRIDLINGTON - HUMBERSIDE
➤ *Landranger 101 GR 190670*

Surf Although not renowned for it's surf, Bridlington does pick up some reasonably good waves on a big swell from the S or SE; the waves will tend to be bigger as you move N towards North Beach. It's a beach break, with peaks breaking both right and left. Best at low tide. A good beach for beginners. Winds from NNW to W are offshore.

Access The A165 runs into Bridlington from the N and S, and the A166 from inland. The route is well-signposted. There is plenty of parking on the seafront and in the town.

Facilities In the summer, Bridlington has everything you're likely to need for a day at the coast - cafes, shops, pubs, amusement arcades, nightlife, etc. If the surf's no good there are plenty of alternatives - you can hire sailboarding and sailing equipment, go water skiing, paragliding, or sea

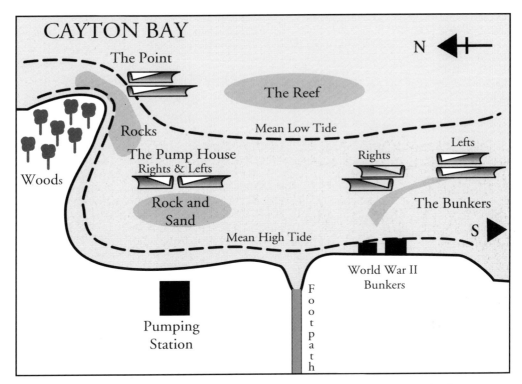

CAYTON BAY

The Point

The Reef

Mean Low Tide

Rocks

The Pump House
Rights & Lefts

Lefts

Rights

Woods

Rock and
Sand

The Bunkers

N

S

Mean High Tide

World War II
Bunkers

Pumping
Station

Footpath

fishing. If the weather's lousy you could try Leisure World, a water sports and entertainment complex. If you want something a little more cultured, try a visit to Sewerby Hall. The choice will probably be more limited in the winter.

Accommodation There are caravan parks and camp sites and cheap hotels in abundance.

5 FILEY - NORTH YORKS
➤ *Landranger 101 GR 120800*

Surf A series of beach breaks, with peaks which occur the length of Filey Bay. As the bay curves round from facing SE to NE, it has the advantage of picking up swells from most directions. The north end at Filey picks up SE and E swells, and the south end, at REIGHTON SANDS, picks up the more frequent NE and N swells. There can be quite strong longshore currents on a big swell. At the S end of the bay SW winds are offshore, at the N end winds from W to NW are offshore. OK for beginners, but bear the currents in mind.

Access Filey is well-signposted from the A165. There's plenty of parking space in pay-and-display car parks and along the promenade. If you want to

surf S of Filey, take the A165 south. There are a number of turn-offs to the bay and Reighton Sands.

Facilities Various kiosks, shops, etc in Filey. Limited facilities if you choose to surf further S in the bay. Filey still retains much of it's old character, with fishermen often to be seen mending their nets at Coble Landing at the N end of town.

Accommodation Holiday camps, caravan parks and camp sites. Good but cheap hotels abound between Bridlington to the S and Scarborough to the N.

6 CAYTON BAY - NORTH YORKS
➤ *Landranger 101 GR 070845*

Surf (See diagram) There are a number of breaks here. At the S end of the bay is a high tide beach break, with lefts and rights; one of the few places in the area that works at high tide.

In the middle of the bay there's a reef break. It needs a big swell to work, and gives both lefts and rights. Best at mid tide.

To the N of this is another reef break, with both lefts and rights; best from mid to low tide.
Right at the N end of the bay, there's a left hander at Osgodby Point. It needs swell of over 5ft to work.

There are also beach breaks inside the reefs along the length of the bay.

On a good swell, you could spend all day surfing here, just moving from one break to another depending on the state of the tide. The bay works best on a N or NE swell, but also picks up big SE swells.

At the S end of Cayton Bay winds from the SW are offshore, with offshores gradually becoming W to NW as you move N up the bay. The beach breaks are OK for beginners, although there are some tricky rips and currents to watch out for. The reef breaks are some way offshore and should be left to experienced surfers only.

Access   The A165 Filey-Scarborough road runs above Cayton Bay. There's a car park above the bay opposite the holiday camp, from where you take a steep path down the cliffs to the beach. You can check out the whole bay from the top of the cliffs before you commit yourself to the steep walk down and stiff climb back.

Facilities   Surf shop in car park with free hot showers. Snacks avialable too. Open everyday in season and in the winter weekends or by arrangement. Professional surf forecast available on 01723 582495.

Accomodation   Holiday camps, caravan parks and camp sites abound. There are also several reasonably-priced hotels in the area.

7 SCARBOROUGH, SOUTH BAY - NORTH YORKS
➤ *Landranger 101 GR 054883*

Surf   South Bay has both a beach break and a reef break, the reef being at the S end of the bay. The beach has peaks along its length on a big N or NE swell. There's often a very obvious increase in the size of the waves from N to S, so you can choose the size of wave to suit you. This means that the reef, a fast right-hander at the S end of the bay, will pick up the most swell. Best from low to mid tide - at high tide you get backwash from the sea wall. This isn't a problem at the N end, which can be surfed right through from low to high tide on a big swell. NW to W winds are offshore.

South Bay is a good place to head for if North Bay is too big. It's also more sheltered than North Bay when the winds have some N in them. The beach is fine for beginners, the reef is best left to experienced surfers.

South Bay, Scarborough

Access   There are four main roads into Scarborough - the A165 from the S and N, the A 171 from the N, and the A170 and A64 from inland. South Bay is well- signposted once you reach the centre of town. There's a car park above the beach, but it's ridiculously expensive, and an underground car park at the roundabout above the beach - this is a good place to change if the weather is bad. The town, beach, and car parks are usually crowded in summer.

Facilities   There is a surf shop (see Appendix), shops, cafes (good fish and chips), and pubs along the beach front and up in the town. There are also amusement arcades and a small fair. Lifeguards operate in the summer. There's plenty to do if the surf is flat - sea fishing trips, big aqua slides at North Bay, and good coastal walks. The North Yorkshire Moors are well worth a visit and offer excellent mountain biking. There's plenty of night life, especially in the summer.

Accommodation   Caravan parks and camp sites, holiday camps, cheap and expensive hotels, the choice is yours. There's also a youth hostel at Scalby, just north of Scarborough.

8 SCARBOROUGH, NORTH BAY - NORTH YORKS
➤ *Landranger 101 GR 040895*

Surf   North Bay picks up more swell than South Bay, mainly from the N, NE, and E, but it will also pick up big SE swells. If South Bay has a small wave, it will usually be much bigger here. When its working well it can produce a surprisingly good wave. The best waves tend to be at the S end of the bay, breaking over sand and rock. The rights are better.

North Bay is only surfable from low to just after mid-tide: after this the backwash off the sea wall messes up the waves. The only way back in at high tide is to make the long paddle up to the N end of the beach. Be aware of the backwash while you're doing this. The north end also has a beach break, which works right through the tide. This is better for beginners than the wave at the S end. SW to W winds are offshore.

Access   See South Bay. There are signs to North Bay once you get into Scarborough. Plenty of parking all along the promenade above the beach, although you have to pay. You can get out to the waves by walking down the steps to the beach and paddling out, or

North Bay, Scarborough

walking through a tunnel under the road at the S end of the bay which brings you out on rocks close to the line up - not recommended for beginners.

Facilities   A snack bar overlooks the break at the N end, and there are a few shops, plus amusements and a leisure park at the S end. Otherwise see South Bay.

Accommodation   See South Bay.

9 SANDSEND - NORTH YORKS
➤ *Landranger 94 GR 870130*

Surf   Sandsend can produce an excellent quality, fast and hollow beach break. There are peaks all along the beach, as far as WHITBY SANDS to the S, which is just an extension of the same beach. (Indeed, there's plenty of scope to explore for reef breaks all the way down to Scarborough - check Robin Hood's Bay, for example). The peaks tend to shift around, and give both lefts and rights. It's usually best from low to mid tide - at high tide there's a tendency for it to close out and dump very heavily on the beach. At the S end towards Whitby there's backwash off the cliffs at high tide. There's a good break at this end of the beach from low to mid

tide known as 'Secrets' near Upgang. It works on any swell, although as it faces NE it's more susceptible to swells from the N and NE. Winds from S through to W are offshore to cross-shore. OK for beginners, although the waves can be surprisingly heavy.

Access   The A174 Whitby-Sandsend road runs alongside the beach. There's parking at the roadside, and a car park above the beach. The Sandsend end of the beach is far more accessible than the Whitby end.

Facilities   Refreshments and toilets available in Sandsend. Plenty of shops, cafes, pubs, etc. in nearby Whitby, which is worth a visit.

Accommodation   There are a number of caravan parks and camp sites both on the coast and just inland. There are youth hostels at Whitby and Boggle Hole near Robin Hood's Bay.

10 CAVES, SANDSEND - NORTH YORKS
➤ *Landranger 94 GR 870312*

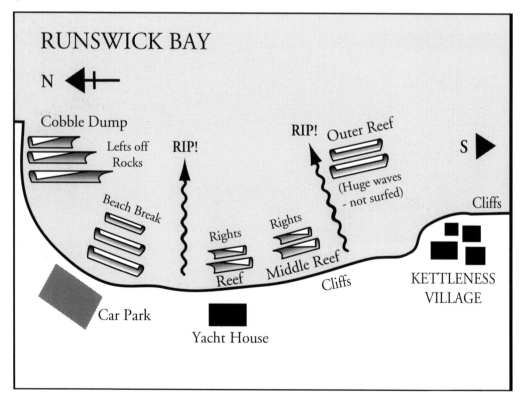

Surf A left hand reef break beneath the cliffs to the N of Sandsend village which is very popular with local surfers, so you may find it somewhat crowded when it's working well. It's best around mid tide, although on a neap tide it will work virtually all the way through. Best on a NW to N swell. SW winds are offshore, but it's well protected from W and NW winds by the cliffs. A pleasant, mellow wave for a reef break, often giving long rides. Not really a beginners wave though.

On a big swell there's also a peak just to the S of Caves, breaking both left and right - it's straight in front of the car park. With both these waves there's a danger of getting trapped if the tide gets too high, as it breaks against the cliffs. In this case the only safe way of getting back in is to make the long paddle S to the beach.

Access Just below the steep hill to the north of Sandsend there's a turn-off from the A174 through a stone arch, right at the N end of the village. Go through this into the car park below the cliffs. From there you climb over the sea wall and paddle out to the break.

Facilities and accommodation See Sandsend.

11 RUNSWICK BAY - NORTH YORKS
➤ *Landranger 94 GR 810160*

Surf (see diagram) There are four potential breaks here, all of which work from low to mid tide, and require a moderate to big N to NW swell.

1. The outer reef below Kettleness village throws up a huge right-hander which, I understand, has yet to be ridden. It will hold waves twice the size of those on the inner reefs.

2. The middle reef, another right-hander, but not as big as the outer reef - there's a strong rip between the middle and outer reef - be careful of this or you could inadvertently find yourself becoming the first person to 'surf' the outer reef.

3. A right-hander in front of the yacht house, a beach break with lefts and rights. The only spot really suitable for beginners. Beware of a rip in the middle of the bay.

4. Cobble Dump, a left-hander breaking over rocks at the N end of the bay.

Winds from S to SW are offshore. Runswick is a good place to head for when the waves everywhere else are too big.

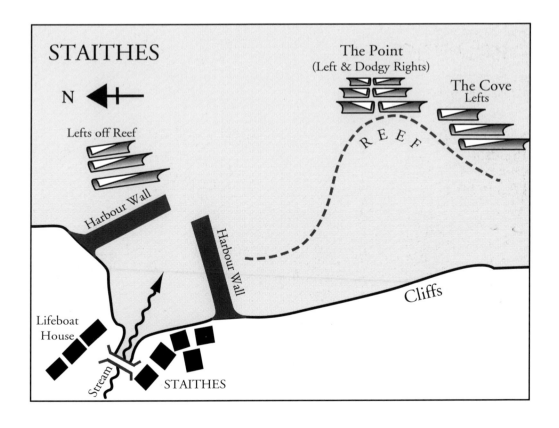

Access Follow the signposts from the A174 coast road. There's a car park at the bottom of the hill down to the bay, which is a picturesque place to spend a few hours surfing.

Facilities Toilets by the car park, cafe and shops in village. Runswick is well placed for walking the Cleveland Way for a few miles in either direction. It takes you along some of the highest and most dramatic cliffs in England, and drops down into some interesting and picturesque old fishing villages.

Accommodation A limited number of caravan parks and camp sites towards Whitby and Guisborough. Youth hostels in Whitby and Brotton.

12 STAITHES - NORTH YORKS
➤ *Landranger 94 GR 784188*

Surf (see diagram) There are three excellent reef breaks here, which are fast, powerful, and hollow, and will hold surfable waves up to 15ft on a solid,

N'ly groundswell. All are low to mid tide breaks because at high tide the sea comes right up to the base of the steep and unstable cliffs above the breaks cutting you off; this is particularly true of the The Point and The Cove. All the waves break on flat wave-cut platforms. Very often there's an abundance of kelp in the line-up which can help to soften the impact of a wipe out, but it clings on to you as you try to extricate yourself from it - not pleasant! From S to N the breaks are as follows:

1. The Cove - A fast, walling left hander, with a fast, peaky take-off, which can give good long rides back into the cove.

2. The Point - A left, and also a short, dodgy, very shallow right. The left is by far the better wave, and is often hollow, with a good clean wall on a well lined-up swell.

3. The Harbour - A bowly left-hand peak in front of the N harbour wall, with a critical take-off.

None of the breaks handle crowds well. S to SW winds are offshore. None of these breaks are suitable for beginners.

There are several wave-cut platform reef breaks to the north of Staithes, beneath the cliffs. They're low to mid tide breaks because you will be cut off by the tide towards high water. Access is difficult, though, and they're rarely, if ever, surfed.

Staithes overview

Access Signs for Staithes from the A174 coast road - watch out for the sign with Captain Cook (who used to sail from here) pointing to the harbour. There's a car park above the village, from where you have a long walk down to the breaks - non-residents' cars are not allowed in the village.

There's also access from the village of Cowbar to the N, but you're likely to get a parking ticket if you leave your car in Staithes using this route.

Facilities Shops, cafes, pubs in Staithes, surf shop in Saltburn, a few miles up the coast.

Accommodation See Runswick Bay.

13 SKINNINGROVE - CLEVELAND
➤ *Landranger 94 GR 714200*

Surf There's a right-hand reef break to the south of Skinningrove village, which is rather fickle, and beach breaks in front of the village. Both work from low to mid tide. At high water the reef is cut off and there's a marked backwash from the cliffs. To the N of the breakwater is a long sandy beach which also has waves. The two beach breaks are OK for beginners. Best on a N to NE swell, but also picks up

a SE and E swell. S to SW winds are offshore.

Access From the A174 take the signposted turn-off down to Skinningrove. Limited parking available in village.

Facilities Shops and pubs in Skinningrove and nearby Loftus. Good fish and chip shop in Skinningrove! Surf shop in Saltburn.

Acommodation See Saltburn.

14 SALTBURN - CLEVELAND
➤ *Landranger 94 GR 668218*

Surf (See diagram) Saltburn is the centre of the surfing scene in North Yorkshire and Cleveland. It's also one of the most crowded spots on the NE coast when there's a good swell running. The locals are a friendly bunch (despite the crowds), and I've always found surfing here to be a pretty cool experience. The breaks are described from S to N:

1. There's a right hand point break on Saltburn Scar, a reef below Huntcliff, which works best at mid tide - at high tide you get cut off by the cliffs.

2. To the N of this is Penny Hole, a good left-

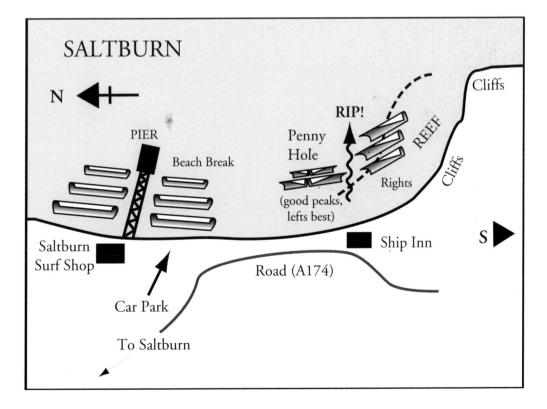

hander, and also good rights at times, breaking over sand. It's best around low tide. There's a strong rip in between Penny Hole and the point break. Pollution is a problem here.

3. To the north again is the main beach, with peaks either side of the pier. It works all through the tide, although it has a tendency to drop off on low tide. On a big swell or a spring high tide, backwash from the seawall can be a problem.

All the breaks work on swells from NW through to SE, although the further south you go along the beach the less chance there is of a SE swell getting in. S to SW winds are offshore. In a strong NW or W wind strong longshore currents can develop. The main beach is ideal for beginners.

Pollution has been a major concern of surfers in Saltburn for some time. Not just the breaks to the S of the bay, but the main beach also is often heavily polluted, and many local surfers have suffered ear, eye, and stomach infections as a result.

Access   The A174 runs alongside the beach, and there's a car park by the pier.

Facilities   The beach is patrolled by lifeguards in summer. There are kiosks selling food and drink by the pier, two pubs above the beach, and plenty of shops and pubs in the town. There is a surf shop literally above the beach and surf reports are available on 01891 545543.

Accommodation   There's a youth hostel in Saltburn, and a caravan park and camp site in between Skelton and Guisborough.

15 REDCAR - CLEVELAND
➤ *Landranger 94 GR 610250*

Surf   Beach breaks exist all the way up from Saltburn, through Marske, to Redcar, and there are good high tide waves off the groynes just to the south of Redcar. Access is over the dunes from the main road (A1085) between Marske and Redcar. There are several breaks in Redcar itself.

1. Off the Shoreline roundabout is a left hand reef break, working from low to mid tide.
2. 200 yards N of (1) are three reef breaks at a spot known as Denny's. The first is a left and right, the next two are both rights.
3. 200 yards further north again is a beach break opposite Leo's nightclub, with lefts and rights from mid tide up.

There are also breaks off the reefs (known locally as scars), which are exposed at low tide, but they're rarely if ever surfed. SW winds are offshore. The beach breaks are OK for beginners.

Access   All these breaks can be reached directly from the A1085 which runs alongside the beach. There's parking at the roadside or in a large car park at the N end of Redcar at the amusement park.

Facilities   Shops, cafes, pubs in Redcar. Also see Saltburn.

Accommodation   See Saltburn.

16 COATHAM SANDS - CLEVELAND
➤ *Landranger 93 GR 570270*

Surf   There are left and right-hand peaks which work right through the tide all the way along the beach up to the breakwater at South Gare. There are also waves off West Scar at the S end of Coatham beach, and a reef break off the South Gare breakwater. This can be a dodgy place to surf, as the waves break over boulders and there are strong currents. SW to W winds are offshore. The beach breaks are OK for beginners.

Access   Roundabouts off the A1085 leads to the beach. Park in the amusement arcade and walk up from there.

Facilities   Refreshments available above the beach and in Coatham and Redcar. Also see Saltburn.

Accommodation   See Saltburn.

17 SOUTH GARE - CLEVELAND
➤ *Landranger 93 GR 555275*

Surf   A right hander in the mouth of the river Tees breaking off a man-made boulder pile upstream of the lighthouse. It's a fast, heavy break, best from mid to high tide. It works on big E and SE swells. Pollution is bad here; you may be able to find cleaner water if you surf on an incoming tide. There's also less likelihood of being troubled by seaward currents then. S to SE winds are offshore. Not a beginner's break.

Access   It's not easily described, you'd be best to use an OS map for accurate details. Park before the lighthouse compound gates and walk over the grass bank to the river mouth.

Facilities & Accommodation   See Coatham Sands.

Brown and murky, fast and furious - The Cove, Staithes

18 SEATON CAREW / HARTLEPOOL - CLEVELAND
➤ *Landranger 93 GR 530291*

Surf This stretch of coast is better exposed to SE swells than anywhere else in the area. It's also sheltered from NW winds. Unfortunately I have little information other than that and the fact that the area has a selection of beach and reef breaks. However, it's a very industrialised area, which detracts somewhat from the surfing to be had here.

Access The A178 runs along the coast through Seaton Carew and into Hartlepool; the A689 and A179 run into Hartlepool from inland.

Facilities Shops, pubs, cafes in both towns. There is a surf shop in Hartlepool (see Appendix).

Accommodation Sparse

19 ROKER BEACH, SUNDERLAND - TYNE AND WEAR
➤ *Landranger 88 GR 409950*

Surf There are left and right-hand peaks on the beach, and a fast right-hander off the harbour wall which can double in size as it breaks. Best from mid to high tide and on a NE to N swell. W to NW winds are offshore. There's a N'ly longshore drift as the swell picks up. The beach is OK for beginners; the harbour wall should be left to more experienced surfers.

Access The A183 coast road runs alongside the beach from the N, and out of the centre of Sunderland, off the A1018, the town's main artery. Park at the side of the road next to the beach.

Facilities Shops, cafes, pubs in town.

Accomodation See South Shields - otherwise very little.

20 SOUTH SHIELDS - TYNE AND WEAR
➤ *Landranger 88 GR 380675*

Surf A beach break with left and right-hand peaks along the the beach. It tends to be better from mid to high tide. It can hold a good-sized wave - over head-high and is best on N, NE, or N swells. The long harbour wall to the north affords some protection from N'ly winds. If South Shields is too small it may be worth checking the breaks to the N of the Tyne. If it's too big, the beaches to the S may

Low tide, Saltburn

have smaller waves. SW winds are offshore. OK for beginners. The water is noticeably cleaner here than that to the north of the Tyne.

Although I have no detailed information on it, MARSDEN, a couple of miles to the S on the A183, also gets surf, and you may find it less crowded than South Shields. It could be worth the short drive to check it out. One of its great advantages is the pub, the 'Grotto', right on the beach - handy for an apres surf pint.

Access The A183 runs along the coast. From the N it's reached via the Tyne Tunnel. From Newcastle or the S it's well signposted from all the major roads. There's a car park above the beach.

Facilities Shops, cafes, and pubs above beach and in the town. Tourist information. There's a skate park next to the beach, and a fairground at the N end. Lifeguards patrol the beach in summer.

Accommodation A caravan park and camp site at Marsden.

21 BLACK MIDDENS - TYNE AND WEAR
➤ *Landranger 88 GR 374869*

Surf A most aptly named break - being inside the mouth of the heavily polluted river Tyne the water

lives up to its name. Swallowing it is not advisable. Black Middens is a left-hand reef break on the N side of the estuary, which can produce fast, very hollow waves on a big E'ly swell. It's best from mid to high tide. It can be a hazardous spot to surf though, as the water is shallow and there are numerous projecting rocks. You also surf directly into the path of oncoming shipping - a head-on collision with one of the North Sea ferries could badly ding your board. Not a beginner's wave.

Access From the A193 into Tynemouth take the turn off to the Collingwood Monument, just past the priory. There's a car park here, from where you walk and clamber down to the break.

Facilities Shops, cafes, pubs in Tynemouth.

Accommodation See Longsands.

22 KING EDWARDS BAY - TYNE AND WEAR
► *Landranger 88 GR 373696*

Surf 'Eddie's Bay' is a small cove, well sheltered from all but E winds by the high cliffs surrounding it. It usually has a peaky beach break in the centre of the bay with subsidiary peaks on either side; these may move around as the sand banks shift. It's best from low to three-quarter tide, and is usually a relatively easy paddle out once past the shore break. It's best on N to NE swells, or a good E swell, accompanied by offshore SW to W winds. OK for beginners.

Access About 200 yards S of Longsands - see Longsands entry for more details.

Facilities Beach cafe/shop in summer. The Gibraltar Rock pub above the beach provides a grandstand view of the surf along with the luxury of a comfortable seat, warm feet, and a pint of bitter. For more details see Longsands.

Accommodation See Longsands.

23 LONGSANDS BAY, TYNEMOUTH - TYNE AND WEAR
► *Landranger 88 GR 368702*

Surf The centre of the Newcastle surfing scene. Longsands is a beach break, with left and right-hand peaks throughout its length. Usually surfed at the S end to avoid rock outcrops and the remains of old sea defences. There can be waves at most stages of the tide, but the best time is just before and just after high water. It can hold a big swell, with surfable waves over head height breaking here. On a big swell there's a rip beside the rocks in front of the open air swimming pool. SW to W winds are offshore. A popular beach with beginners.

Access The A1058 from Newcastle goes to Tynemouth, and the A193 from Whitley Bay runs above the beach. There's limited parking on the slipway to the beach and parking on the road, otherwise there's a car park above King Edward's Bay or you can try the side streets.

Facilities and Accommodation Shops, cafes and public toilets on the beach in summer. There are also plenty of shops, cafes and pubs in nearby Tynemouth town centre plus a surf shop in North Shields (see Appendix). Lifeguards and surf hire on the beach in summer.

24 WHITLEY BAY - TYNE AND WEAR
► *Landranger 88 GR 354730*

Surf A beach break, with left and right-hand peaks, but there are occasional rock outcrops to watch out for. Local surfers seem to prefer Longsands though. The most popular spot tends to be off the promenade which works best from mid to high tide and is better on N or E swells. SW to W winds are offshore. OK for beginners.

Access From Newcastle the A191 and the A1058 are signposted for the coast and Whitley Bay/Tynemouth. From the N the A193 coast road runs through the town and down to Tynemouth. There's a one way system through the centre. Park in side streets off the beach. There are car parks above the beach at the N end. It gets crowded in summer.

Facilities Whitley Bay has it all - in summer anyway. There's a fun fair, amusement arcades, candy floss, pubs and cafes, the lot.

Accommodation Caravan park to the north.

25 HARTLEY REEF - TYNE AND WEAR
► *Landranger 88 GR 346757*

Surf Hartley is a favourite break with Geordie surfers, who will tell you with good reason that, on its day, it compares with any wave in the country. It's a fast, hollow, and powerful reef break and is one of the most consistent spots in the area - it will always be a couple of feet bigger than the surrounding beach breaks. Hartley picks up most swells, particularly those from the E and NE. It works from mid to high tide, with both rights and lefts at mid tide, although the right fades as the tide rises. It will work from 3ft to 10ft or more. Winds from SW to W are offshore. The reef is a flat rock slab about 400 yards out to sea, with few projections, so it's fairly user-friendly. However, it's not a beginner's wave.

Access At the junction of the A193 coast road and the B1325 there's a roundabout with a turn-off down a short road to the coast above the break. The reef is on the left as you look out to sea from the cliffs. There are steps down the cliff, from where you make the long paddle out to the break.

Facilities The Hartley Inn by the roundabout sells good beer and bar snacks. Otherwise the nearest facilities are in Seaton or Whitley Bay. Plenty of pubs for the evening's entertainment in Whitley Bay and Tynemouth.

Accommodation There's a small caravan site next to the car park, and a larger one to the N of Whitley Bay.

26 SEATON SLUICE - NORTHUMBERLAND
➤ *Landranger 88 GR 332772*

Surf A beach break, with left and right-hand peaks along its length, which vary with the shifting sands. It picks up N and NE swells, which tend to be larger as you move S down the beach. Large SE to S swells will get into the N end of the beach. Best from mid to three-quarter tide. A good beginner's beach.

Access The A193 runs alongside the beach. There are car parks next to the road, and short paths run through the dunes to the beach.

Facilities Toilets in the car park, shops in the town.

Accommodation See Blyth.

27 BLYTH, SOUTH HARBOUR - NORTHUMBERLAND
➤ *Landranger 81 GR 322800*

Surf Blyth is a beach break, both lefts and rights, which are often quite long. It's well sheltered by the harbour wall from northerly winds, and works well on a big N or NE swell. It will also pick up large S to SE swells. If it's too big or messy at the popular nearby breaks around Tynemouth it's often worth checking Blyth. There's a cross shore current from N-S on a big swell. Best on winds from W to NW. A popular beach with sailboarders. Birth place of former world surfing champion Martin Potter.

Access Take the A193 coast road into Blyth, and turn right at the roundabout at Newsham, following signs to the beach. There's plenty of parking above the beach.

Facilities Vans above the beach in summer providing refreshments. Plenty of shops, cafes, and pubs in town.

Accommodation Caravan sites at Wansbeck.

Making the most of a North Sea swell

estuary and in Whitley Bay. There's a small caravan site above Hartley Reef.

28 WANSBECK ESTUARY - NORTHUMBERLAND
➤ *Landranger 81 GR 304854*

Surf Two river mouth breaks either side of the estuary, both breaking into the river mouth - the N side has a right and the S has a left. They both break over sand and both jack up nicely to give a good peak on most swells. At low tide it's more of a beach break with the two seperate peaks developing as the tide rises. Winds from the W are offshore. OK for beginners, but watch out for the seaward flow of the river on an outgoing tide, especially if there's been heavy rain. You may find the water is slightly warmer here than elsewhere on the coast - a result of outflow from the nearby power station.

Access Park in the caravan site above the beach - directly off the A189.

Facilities Food and drink may be available at the caravan site, otherwise you'll have to go into one of the nearby towns.

Accommodation There's the Sandy Bay caravan site by the river in summer, otherwise little else unless you go inland to the more touristy spots such as Morpeth, or up the coast to Druridge Bay.

29 HORSE HEAD REEF - NORTHUMBERLAND
➤ *Landranger 81 GR 314870*

Surf A predominantly left-hand reef break to the N of the Wansbeck estuary. It holds big swells from any direction, and is usually bigger than surrounding breaks. It's more or less just a big drop which then quickly backs off as it breaks in deep water, in channels either side of the reef. Best from low to mid tide. At high tide the sea comes up to the cliffs, so make sure you get out of the water in plenty of time. W winds are offshore. It's a 20-minute paddle out to the wave, so you're on your own if you get into difficulty - clearly a wave for experienced surfers only.

Access The A189 crosses the mouth of the Wansbeck, just after which you turn off onto the minor road to Newbiggin. Park just after the junction, from where you have to walk to the break.

You'll need an OS map to find its location accurately.

Facilities None at the break. Shops and pubs abound in all the nearby towns - Newbiggin, Ashington, Blyth. Morpeth is by far the most pleasant to visit, about seven miles inland.

Accommodation See Wansbeck Estuary.

30 CHURCH POINT, NEWBIGGIN - NORTHUMBERLAND
➤ *Landranger 81 GR 318879*

Surf An infrequently surfed right-hand reef break which works on a N or E swell, or a very big one from the SE. Best from low to three-quarter tide. W to SW winds are offshore. Not a beginner's wave.

Access The A197 runs into Newbiggin; Church Point is out past the lifeboat station.

Facilities Shops, cafes and pubs in Newbiggin.

Accommodation See Wansbeck Estuary.

31 LYNEMOUTH BEACH - NORTHUMBERLAND
➤ *Landranger 81 GR 303915*

Surf One of the least recommended spots in the book unless you enjoy surfing in liquid coal. The water here is literally black, as is the beach, from coal dust washed from waste tips lining the beach. If you must surf here, you'll find a number of peaks breaking on rock slab reefs along the length of the beach. The waves break in shallow water and are best at high tide. There's a strong N to S longshore current. SW to W winds are offshore. Not recommended for beginners - or anyone else for that matter.

Access From the A1069 follow signs along the minor road, or follow signs off the A197 from Newbiggin - or just head for the chimneys of the aluminium smelters in the town. Park above the beach. Lock any valuables in the car.

Facilities Shops and very local pubs in town. Free coal on beach.

Accommodation See Druridge Bay.

32 WHITE POLE - NORTHUMBERLAND
➤ *Landranger 81 GR 302927*

Surf A reef break about 250 yards out to sea. It has a strong N to S longshore current running across the break. There are lefts and rights, generally best surfed on an outgoing tide from three-quarter to mid tide as the current tends to be stronger when the tide's coming in. Winds from W are offshore. Be careful of shallow water on the inside otherwise you risk losing fins and skin on the reef. Not a beginner's wave.

Access, Facilities and Accommodation See Snab Point and Druridge Bay.

33 SNAB POINT -
➤ *Landranger 81 GR 303927*

Surf This is the headland to the S of Creswell. It's another reef break, just to the N of Snab Point, with lefts and rights, best between mid and three-quarter tide. Watch out for a N to S longshore current when the swell has some size. Winds from W are offshore. Not a beginner's wave.

Access Take the coast road S from Creswell for about 3/4 mile, or N from Lynemouth. Park at side of road above break. There are reports of vehicles being broken into on the stretch of coast between here and Lynemouth, so hide your valuables.

Facilities Shops selling refreshments above beach in summer, cafe in Creswell, or you could try Lynemouth.

Accommodation See Druridge Bay.

34 CRESWELL BEACH - NORTHUMBERLAND
➤ *Landranger 81 GR 295935*

Surf This is really the southern extension of Druridge Bay, and has left and right hand peaks which are often working when other beaches in the area are flat. It's quite a mellow wave, working best from three-quarter to high tide. SW winds are offshore. There are no real problems with rips unless the swell gets big, so it's OK for beginners.

Embleton Bay, Northumberland

There's also a reef break here on Creswell Scars, with both lefts and rights breaking on the flat rock slabs that make up the Scars. It picks up more swell than the beach and can get very hollow. Best from mid to high tide. This is not a beginner's wave.

Access Signposts to Creswell from the A1068. There's a large car park above the beach.

Facilities and Accommodation See Druridge Bay.

35 DRURIDGE BAY - NORTHUMBERLAND
➤ *Landranger 81 GR 275980*

Surf A five-mile crescent of golden sands backed by dunes, with rock outcrops at either end. The S end faces NE and thus picks up the most swell, but the N end is OK on a big S or SE swell. There are beach breaks throughout the length of the beach giving good lefts and rights. The peaks tend to shift as the banks move about. It's best from three-quarter to high tide. SW to NW winds are offshore. OK for beginners.

Access As the surf is generally better at the S end of the bay the best bet is to take the turn-off to Creswell at the signposted roundabout on the A1068. The road runs into Creswell and above the beach for a couple of miles. Parking is available above the beach.

Facilities There are ice cream vans above the beach in summer and a cafe in Creswell. There are nature reserves at Druridge, Hauxley and Coldrife Country Park at the N end of the bay.

Accommodation There are a number of caravan sites in the area.

36 ALN ESTUARY - NORTHUMBERLAND
➤ *Landranger 81 GR 248102*

Surf A rivermouth break with left and rights breaking over a sand bottom to either side of the Aln estuary. It's best from three-quarter to high tide, and is offshore in a NW to W wind. Watch out for seaward currents from the river flowing out to sea as the tide drops; particularly after heavy rains. OK for beginners as long as you watch out for the currents.

There are also peaks either side of the estuary along the length of Alnmouth Bay.

Access The A1068 coast road runs to the W of Alnmouth with a turn-off to the village and beach. Drive S through the village to the rivermouth. There's a car park above the beach.

Facilities Shops, cafes, and pubs in the village of Alnmouth 1.5 miles away. It's a picturesque, unspoilt village which is well worth a visit. The pubs are good.

Accommodation Not a great deal in the immediate vicinity. There is a caravan park and camp site to the N at Embleton, and a youth hostel at Rock.

Although I have little information, I know that the stretch of coastline between Alnmouth in the S and Beadnell to the N is well worth exploring for new breaks. There's heaps of potential for finding quiet, isolated reef and beach breaks for yourself, as there are few surfers in this area. A couple of examples are FOOTBALL HOLE, a reef break just south of Dunstanburgh Castle, and the little fishing villages of CRASTER and BOULMER, which both have beach breaks.

37 EMBLETON BAY - NORTHUMBERLAND
➤ *Landranger 75 GR 245230*

Surf Another fine sweeping crescent-shaped beach, with golden sands and the brooding ruins of Dunstanburgh Castle on the craggy headland to the south. It has beach break peaks along its length giving rights and lefts which can provide pretty long rides. Works at all stages of the tide. The N end picks up more S and SE swell, the S end picks up more N swell. Winds from SE to NW are offshore depending which end of the beach you're at. OK for beginners. Embleton is a beach that's well worth a visit even if the surf is flat.

Access From the B1340 take the minor road to High Newton then Low Newton, where you can park and walk south along a path to the beach. There's also access to the middle of the beach from the B1339 through Embleton and down to the sea. There's a car park by the golf course.

Facilities See Low Newton. The Embleton car park has no facilities, the nearest are in the village and are limited.

Accommodation See Beadnell Bay

38 LOW NEWTON - NORTHUMBERLAND
➤ Landranger 75 GR 243245

Surf I have little information on the surf here other than that it's a beach break on a small E facing beach.

Access From High Newton-by-the-Sea follow signs along minor road to Low Newton. Car park in village.

Facilities Toilets above beach. Pub at High Newton.

Accommodation See Beadnell Bay.

39 BEADNELL BAY - NORTHUMBERLAND
➤ Landranger 75 GR 230275

Surf A sweeping two mile crescent of sand backed by dunes, this is another of the North East's superb but relatively unknown beaches. The N end of the bay is a reef break, which is SE-facing so more exposed to less frequent S'ly swells, while the S end is a beach break which faces NE and picks up N'ly swells. OK for beginners provided that you keep an eye open for for rips on the outgoing tide.

Access There are minor roads off the B1340 coast road to Beadnell Harbour at the N end of the bay and to High Newton-by-the-Sea at the S end. Car parking above the beach at both ends.

Facilities Ice cream van in N car park in summer. Toilets. Sailboard hire. Pub at High Newton. Otherwise you have to rely on shops in Beadnell.

Accommodation Caravan parks and camp sites at Beadnell and Seahouses; youth hostel at Rock.

40 BAMBURGH - NORTHUMBERLAND
➤ Landranger 75 GR 180355

Surf This is probably one of the most dramatic surf spots in England. The huge pile of Bamburgh Castle towers 150ft above the beach and overlooks the surf. Out at sea to the east are the Farne Islands, and to the north Holy Island, an early Christian retreat with a ruined 11th century priory. Lindisfarne Castle dominates the Holy Island skyline. The whole area is steeped in atmosphere and history, and whether there's surf or not it's a stretch of coastline well worth seeing. The coast at Bamburgh faces NE, so tends to pick up more swell than the E-facing beaches further down the coast. The best waves are usually immediately N of the castle. Here you'll find beach breaks with lefts and rights breaking in clear unpolluted water (it's not unusual to see seals in the line up, or even dolphins and porpoises).

There's surf along the beach down to Seahouses four miles to the S. It works at all stages of the tide and overhead waves are not uncommon. There are no bad rips unless the swell gets large, so it's OK for beginners. SW winds are offshore.

Access There's a coast road, the B1340, running right through Bamburgh. It joins the B1341 and B1342 to the W of the village. Both connect with the A1 some five miles W. There's a car park in the dunes above the beach to the N of the castle, where the best waves are usually found.

Facilities Shops, cafe, hotel and toilets in village, ice cream vans in car parks above beach.

Accommodation Plenty of caravan parks and camp sites in the area.

Holy Island may also be worth a visit if you really go for isolated surf spots. There are definitely waves here, but I have no detailed information.

41 BERWICK-UPON-TWEED
➤ Landranger 75, GR 005521

Surf On a big swell there's an excellent left-hander to be found breaking over a sand bar on the S side of the mouth of the river Tweed. Winds from a W'ly direction are offshore. Paddle out in the river mouth, but beware of currents. Not recommended for inexperienced surfers.

Access The A1167 turn-off from the A1 goes into Berwick. Park above the river mouth.

Facilities Plenty of shops, cafes and pubs in the town. If there's no surf, the superb Border country is to be found inland: it's well worth a visit either by car, foot or mountain bike.

Accommodation There are a number of caravan sites in the town.

The atmospheric Northumberland coast

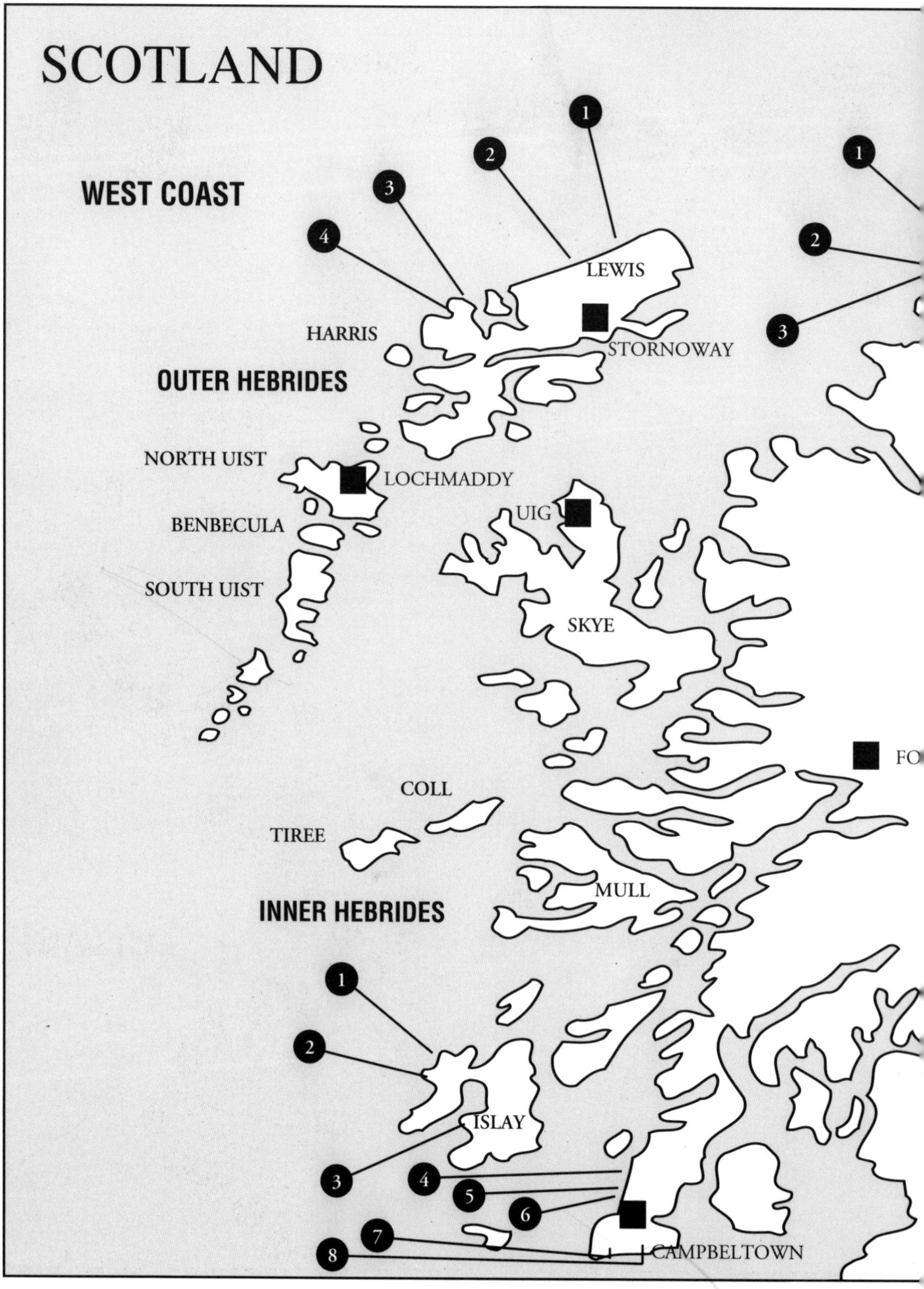

SCOTLAND

WEST COAST

OUTER HEBRIDES

INNER HEBRIDES

LEWIS

STORNOWAY

HARRIS

NORTH UIST

LOCHMADDY

BENBECULA

SOUTH UIST

UIG

SKYE

COLL

TIREE

MULL

FO

ISLAY

CAMPBELTOWN

1
2
3
4

1
2
3

1
2
3
4
5
6
7
8

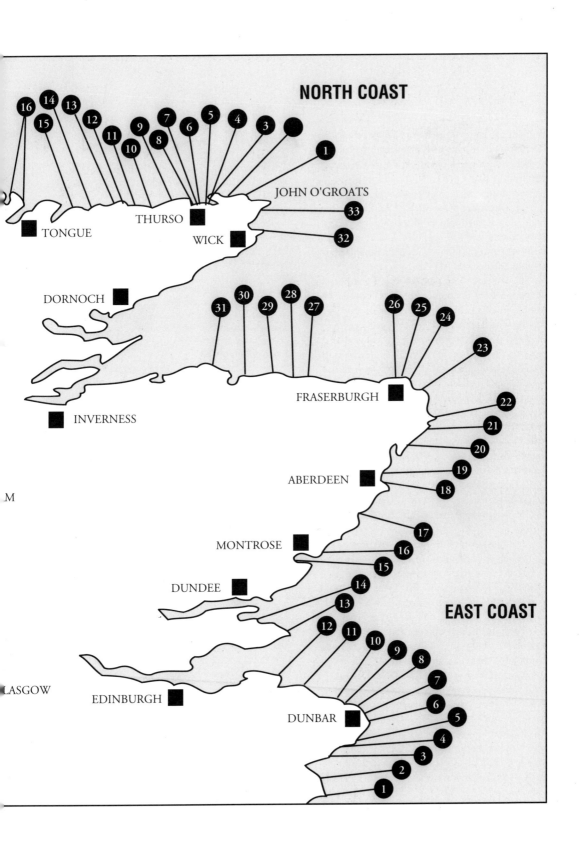

8 SCOTLAND

Scotland can justly lay claim to having the biggest, the best, and the most consistent surf in Britain - and the coldest water. However, the low water temperature hasn't prevented the area from becoming something of a mecca for many British surfers. Those who make the long journey north will find a unique environment in which to surf - big, fast, powerful reef and beach breaks and superb unspoilt scenery, and, in summer, the chance to surf until midnight.

The east coast has a number of very good breaks all the way from the Border to John O'Groats. The south west coast, although less accessible, can also produce good quality surf. It's the north coast, however, that is best known for the quality and consistency of its surf. If you really want to surf in splendid isolation you can get away from it all in every sense of the word by visiting the Western Isles, where crystal clear waters and pristine beaches remain virtually unsurfed, and uncrowded conditions are guaranteed. The islands protect large areas of the coastline on the mainland from swells, so despite the fantastic scenery to be found here, it's a waste of time looking for waves.

Pollution is rarely a problem at most of the breaks in Scotland, particularly as you get further N and W, where you'll find some of the cleanest seas in Britain.

The same low pressure systems that provide surf for the SW of England and Wales, and the east coast of England, also produce surf in Scotland that is often bigger and more powerful. These emanate from Atlantic lows that move in from the west, pass to the north of Scotland, and then track off towards Norway, ensuring that the west and north coasts pick up the swell before the east coast. Swells in the North Sea tend to be short lived (three days or so) compared to those of the north and west, but this coast has the advantage of having prevailing offshore winds. The east coast will also get surf from lows in the southern North Sea and the English Channel which give south-easterly winds in the North Sea, and from low pressure systems anchored over Scandinavia, or up in the Arctic Ocean, sending clean groundswells down from the north.

CLIMATE

Any surfer visiting Scotland is bound to ask, "Just how cold is it?" Considering that Thurso is as far north as Alaska, that's not an entirely unreasonable question but it's probably not as cold as you think.

Average air temperatures for Edinburgh in the SE of the country are as follows: winter 6°C (43°F) high, 2°C (35°F) low, spring 10-4°C (50°-39° F), late summer 18-11°C (64 -52°F), autumn 12-6°C (53-44 °F).

Generally speaking the water gradually gets colder as you move from the south west to north west coast, along the north coast, then down the east coast. Average water temperatures in winter vary between 4-7°C (40-42°F), and in summer between 13-16°C (55-60°F).

For the best combination of surf and weather, the time to visit is late summer to early autumn, when the air temperatures are still reasonably mild, the sea's at its warmest, and the first of the big autumn swells are beginning to roll in.

Winter has the most consistent and biggest waves (15ft or more on the north coast is not at all uncommon). But the cold is a very serious consideration then and restricts the amount of time you can stay in the water as well as the number of sessions you can fit into one day. Also, daylight hours are short - eight hours at most. Conversely, in mid-summer you can theoretically surf for up to 21-22 hours a day in the far north.

Tidal ranges are large and must be taken into account. Some breaks may be totally flat at one stage of the tide and four feet at another. If a break is recommended as being best at high tide make sure that you're there at that time as there may be no wave at all at mid or low tide.

There is little point in surfing in Scotland unless you've got a really good wetsuit. In winter you'll need a full winter steamer (5mm thick at least), boots, gloves, and a hat. In summer, if you're not used to cold water, you'll probably still feel more comfortable in a winter steamer and boots. One last point, if you're camping in Scotland in summer, make sure you are well provided with mosquito coils and a good insect repellent. The midges can be hell.

I've divided Scotland into three sections - East Coast, North Coast, and West Coast, describing the breaks in an anti-clockwise direction starting from the Border area of the East coast.

EAST COAST

A glance at the map will show you that the following areas are well positioned to pick up swells from the N, NE, E, and in some cases the NW:

1. Pease Bay area.
2. St Andrews area.
3. between Fraserburgh and Lossiemouth.
4. North of Wick.

Big SE swells will also get to the beaches on the SE coast. The beaches in the named four areas are the most consistent on the E coast as they generally face N or NE, the direction from which come the more consistent and usually bigger swells.

The rest of the breaks on the E coast, from Arbroath to Peterhead, and from Brora to Helmsdale, face SE and are better positioned to pick up swells from the S, SE, and E.

There is a relatively small but active surfing population on the SE coast between Eyemouth and North Berwick. North of this surfers are something of a rare breed and tend to be found in small clusters at St Andrews, Aberdeen, and Fraserburgh.

1 EYEMOUTH
➤ *Landranger 67 GR 945645*

Surf A beach break with lefts and rights, in the town. Only works from low to mid tide as it breaks into the sea wall at high tide. SW to S winds are offshore. Watch out for a strong rip across the harbour mouth on a falling tide. The beach is OK for beginners.

Access From the A1107 coast road there's a turn-off down the B6355 to Eyemouth. Park above the beach.

Facilities Shops, pubs, etc in the town.

Accommodation There's a caravan park at the W end of the bay, and more caravan parks and camp sites at Coldingham. There's a youth hostel at Coldingham.

2 COLDINGHAM BAY
➤ *Landranger 67 GR 918665*

Surf There's a reef and sandbar at the S end of this picturesque little bay which can produce a good wave, particularly on a N swell. It tends to close out if the swell gets too big. It also picks up waves on a SE swell. Best from mid to high tide. NW winds are offshore. There's a useful rip at the N end of the beach for paddling out, but it should not be used by inexperienced surfers. OK for beginners in moderate conditions.

Access At the end of a minor road off the B6438, which joins up with the A1107. There's a car park above the beach.

Facilities The beach is patrolled by lifeguards in the summer. Cafe off the path to the beach. The Smugglers Hotel. Toilets in car park. The impressive cliffs of St Abb's Head are just to the N. The area is a nature reserve owned by the National Trust and is well worth a visit for the spectacular scenery.

Accommodation See Eyemouth.

3 PEASE BAY
➤ *Landranger 67 GR 795710*

Surf The most popular break in the area, and one of the most consistent as it faces NE and is well-placed to pick up most swells. It is likely to be the most crowded break on this stretch of coast if there'e a swell running. A wave breaks over the boulder reef at the S end of the bay, and there's a beach break over sand in the middle of the beach. The reef is best on a N swell at high tide and on a SE swell at mid to low tide. S to SW winds are offshore. The beach is OK for beginners. The reef, although not exceptionally hazardous, is best left to experienced surfers.

Access A sharp right turn (if you're travelling N) off the A1 at Cocksburnpath leads to the beach. There's car parking above the beach.

Facilities There is a huge caravan park which takes up most of the area behind the beach; there's a chip shop, retaurant and bar on the site. A stream in the middle of the beach is useful for rinsing off your wetsuit. Toilets at car park. The proprietors of the Pease Bay Caravan Park (Cockburnspath) will provide a surf check if you ring them on 0368 830206, there's a good rapport between site owners and surfers.

Accommodation Apart from the caravan park at the bay there's another one and a camp site at White Sands. (Also see Eyemouth).

4 THORNTONLOCH
➤ Landranger 67 GR 755740

Surf A beach break with good lefts and rights from mid to high tide. There's a strong longshore current, especially on bigger swells - beginners in particular should watch out for this. Best in W winds which are offshore. This pleasant stretch of coastline is marred by the looming bulk of Torness nuclear power station.

Access Take the minor road off the A1 just W of the nuclear power station. Park by the caravans on the beach and walk down to the break from there.

Facilities None at the beach, the nearest are in the village. More comprehensive facilities are at Dunbar.

Accommodation See Pease Bay.

5 CHAPEL POINT
➤ Landranger 67 GR 743758

Surf A left-hand point break which requires a big swell of at least 8ft to work. It then produces a very good, fast, hollow wave. Best from mid to high tide. SW to W winds are offshore. There are strong rips to watch out for: not a beginner's wave.

Access Take the road off the A1 just past the power station, then turn right down the road marked 'Private, no construction traffic'. The farmer who owns the land has given surfers permission to use his road, so treat the place with respect. Park above the beach. (A good map is recommended to find your way to this break).

Facilities None.

Accommodation See Pease Bay and Dunbar.

6 WHITE SANDS
➤ Landranger 67 GR 713774

Surf There are two reef breaks here, the better of the two giving long lefts between low and mid tide. SW to W winds are offshore. There's a very bad rip on outgoing tides making it inadvisable to surf here at that time. Another break for experienced surfers only. Pease Bay must be overhead before there's a decent wave here.

Access Further along the same turn-off from the A1 that you take to Chapel Point. Follow signs to Barns Ness, towards the lighthouse. There's parking above the beach.

Facilities Toilets above beach. Nearest shops are in Dunbar.

Accommodation There's a camp site above the beach and caravan parks and camp sites in Dunbar.

7 DUNBAR
➤ Landranger 67 GR 682790

Surf Dunbar has surf on the beaches either side of the town and a reef-break over rocks in the town. The town break has good rights from mid to high tide. Winds from SW to W are offshore. The town break is not suitable for beginners, who should also be very wary of strong rips and currents around the mouth of the river Tyne when surfing the northern beach-break. (Dunbar may have a surfable wave when a big swell is closing out other spots).

Access The A1087 runs from the A1 through Dunbar and alongside both beaches. Park above the breaks.

Facilities Shops, cafes, pubs, in the town.

Accommodation A caravan park and camp site in Dunbar.

8 BELHAVEN BAY
➤ Landranger 67 GR 655790

Surf A beach break with peaks all along, which works best on a N to NE swell. SW winds are offshore. OK for beginners, but beware of bad rips on a big swell. Other local breaks are almost always better.

Access Belhaven is directly W of Dunbar and reached on the A1087. There's ample parking above the bay.

Facilities Toilets at most westerly car park. Some refreshments available at the beach - follow signs for John Muir Country Park.

Accommodation See Dunbar.

9 PEFFER SANDS
➤ *Landranger 67 GR 623825*

Surf A somewhat isolated beach with difficult access, but you'll find a good beach break here, particularly on a SE swell. SW to W winds are offshore. Not an ideal spot for beginners because of its isolation.

Access You will need a good map to find your way here. Take the minor road to the E off the A178 N of Whitekirk - the one marked 'No Access to Beach'! You drive through a number of farms to reach the beach.

Facilities None.
Accommodation Caravan parks and camp sites at North Berwick and Haddington. Otherwise see Dunbar.

10 NORTH BERWICK (EAST BAY)
➤ *Landranger 66 GR 558856*

Surf A north-facing reef break that gives quality lefts which tend to be best on big northerly swells. Best from mid to high tide. S winds are offshore. There can be very bad rips on the outgoing tide - watch out for this. Definitely not a beginner's break. If the red flag is flying, stay out of the water. On big swells, there's often a break to the east of N. Berwick at SEACLIFF BAY. North Berwick, however, is usually better.

Access The A198 runs through the town from where there's access to the break.

Facilities There's everything you're likely to need in the town and more facilities in nearby Edinburgh.

Accommodation There's a caravan park and camp site just to the E of North Berwick near the break and sites can be found dotted around inland. This stretch of coast is within easy reach of Edinburgh, where there's plenty of accommodation. Edinburgh's well worth a visit for both culture and nightlife; particularly if you're in the area during the Edinburgh Festival in August - don't miss it!

11 YELLOWCRAIG BEACH
➤ *Landranger 66 GR 525856*

Surf An option if North Berwick is too big or closed out, this is a right hand point break. It works on very big NE through to SE swells. S to SE winds are offshore. Not really a beginner's break.

Access Get the map out again! Take the A198 from North Berwick to Dirleton, and turn N on a minor road at Dirleton to Yellowcraig Plantation. Park on the seaward side of the plantation and walk over the dunes to the beach.

Facilities None. See North Berwick.

Accommodation Caravan park close to beach. See North Berwick.

12 GULLANE BAY

Surf A superb beach, often seen on TV as it backs on to Muirfield Golf Course. Unfortunately it only works occasionally, perhaps two or three times a year. It faces NW and requires a very big swell to get going. The most likely time to get waves here is during the winter. There's an excellent right-hand point break at the NE end of the beach when it is working, and inferior beach breaks on the main beach - these are OK for beginners, the point break is best left to experienced surfers. SE winds are offshore. There's a strong W'ly rip on big swells.

Access The A198 runs through Gullane, from where you turn off to the beach and park 200 yards above it.

Facilities Lifeguards in summer. Toilet block at centre of beach. Nearest refreshments are in Gullane.

Accommodation See North Berwick.

The next surfable stretch of coastline is to be found to the north of the Firth of Forth.

13 CAMBO SANDS
➤ *Landranger 59 GR 605122*

Surf Cambo Sands is a beach break, facing NE, with peaks up and down its length. It only works on a big swell though. SW winds are offshore. OK for beginners.

On an extremely large SE swell, you may come across a wave further down the coast at KIRKALDY, where there's a beach break in the town. It doesn't often work though, and is rarely surfed.

Access Turn E off the A917 at Kingsbarn, and take the minor road to the coast. There's parking and a picnic site to the north of the beach.

Facilities Nearest are in Kingsbarn or just up the coast at St Andrews.

Accommodation There are caravan parks and camp sites at Crail and St Andrews.

14 ST ANDREWS
➤ Landranger 59 GR 519166

Surf There are two breaks at St Andrews(where there is a surf club), which is better known for its golf course and university than its surf. The harbour has a good left breaking over a sandbar. WEST SANDS is a magnificent stretch of beach backed by the five golf courses of the Royal and Ancient, and has good left and right-hand peaks all the way along that work right through the tides. The only snag with the breaks at St Andrews is that they require a big swell to produce any waves at all. On a swell producing six to eight feet waves at Pease Bay, for instance, St Andrews will only be four to five feet.

W to SW winds are offshore. West Sands in particular is a good beginner's beach, although don't get too near to the mouth of the river Eden at the N end of the beach, as there can be strong currents here.

Access All coast roads in Fife seem to lead to St Andrews. You'll have no problem finding it, as it's well signposted from as far away as the M90 and Edinburgh. Parking is limited in the town, but there's a 1000-space car park at West Beach.

Facilities Refreshments close to West Sands and in the town. Toilets close to the beach. Sailboard hire available at West Sands. If it's flat, take a walk around St Andrews - it's steeped in history, with a 12th century church and cathedral, a 13th century castle, the oldest university in Scotland (founded 1411), and the world famous golf club, founded in 1754. If you're interested in something a little more 20th century, there's a new leisure centre at East Beach.

Accommodation Caravan parks and camp sites around St Andrews.

15 LUNAN BAY
➤ Landranger 54 GR 690500

Surf A crescent-shaped, two-mile long beach which tends to be rather better than the beaches to the S around St Andrews. The N end of the beach (which is the most accessible) picks up SE and S swells; the S end is better on N and NE swells. There are beach breaks throughout the length of the bay which work at all stages of the tide. Winds from SW to NW are offshore. Avoid surfing near the salmon nets to be found at certain points on the beach.

Access There are minor roads off the A92 coast road to Redcastle, Lunan, and Braehead above the bay. The easiest access is from Lunan village where there's a private road with public access to a car park above the beach. Park here and walk over the dunes to the beach. If you want to surf at the S end of the beach I'd recommend checking access on the relevant OS map.

Facilities None - the nearest shops, pubs, and cafes are about three miles away in Montrose.

Accommodation The nearest caravan parks and camp sites are in Arbroath and Montrose.

16 MONTROSE
➤ Landranger 54 GR 728580

Surf The beach at Montrose stretches N for some 2.5 miles from the mouth of the river Esk and forms part of the St Cyrus National Nature Reserve. It has peaks along its length. The S end faces directly E and is better exposed to E, NE and big N swells than the N end, which faces ESE and picks up swells from the S, SE and E. Best from low to mid tide. Winds from W to NW are offshore. OK for beginners, but keep away from the river mouth where there can be very strong currents.

Beyween St Cyrus, at the N end of the beach, and Stonehaven some twelve miles further north, there are a number of reef breaks which offer plenty of scope for exploration. They would probably be at their best on a SE or E swell, or a big N swell. Access is from small side roads from the A92 down to tiny fishing villages.

Access Easy access from the town although as you move north there are fewer roads down to the beach. You can get to the beach at Nether Warburton from a side road off the A92. There's a car park above the beach and boardwalks down to the shore.

Facilities   Shops, pubs, cafes in Montrose, but nothing further up the beach. If you're into wildlife the area will be of interest as the nature reserve has a wide variety of habitats - cliffs, dunes, salt marsh and beach - and some 47 species of bird breed here. More than 300 species of wild flowers have been recorded in the area. You may see grey seals out at sea.

Accomodation   Caravan park in Montrose. Further N there are caravan parks and camp sites in St Cyrus, Johnshaven, and Inverbie.

17 STONEHAVEN
➤ Landranger 45 GR 890868

Surf   There are numerous reefs in this area, and from here on up to Aberdeen. All I discovered about the reefs around Stonehaven is that they work from mid to high tide on a big swell from E through to S.

Access   There's a road off the A92 into Stonehaven where there's plenty of parking on the seafront. The A92 also runs along the coast above the other reef breaks to the N, with turn-offs at intervals down to small harbours.

Facilities   There are ample refreshment facilities in Stonehaven, but this won't be the case further up the coast. The coastline around here is spectacular with impressive Dunnottar Castle to the south perched on cliffs above the sea and interesting geology to the north around Muchalls where the cliffscape boasts stacks, arches, caves, and even an underground waterfall.

Accommodation   Caravan park in Stonehaven.

18 ABERDEEN

Surf   There are three breaks in Aberdeen, about which I have limited information. But I'm sure the small group of local surfers based in Aberdeen would be willing to supply additional advice to travelling surfers. The University also has a surf club and there's a surf shop 'Granite Reef'. See Appendix.

NIGG BAY has some reasonable-looking waves, but the area is not recommended as it's the site of the city's main sewage outfall.

The HARBOUR MOUTH can produce a good right, but it is illegal to surf here.

The best bet, then, is TOWN BEACH, which stretches for some 15 miles N from Aberdeen. Groynes have been erected to prevent sand erosion,

and you get lefts and rights breaking off these. They are often of good quality and can be quite hollow at times. Waves also break on sandbars some 100 yards or so offshore. There's surf all through the tide, although just before and after high tide tends to be best - the paddle out at low tide can be difficult. Winds from the W are offshore. OK for beginners, but there is often a strong longshore rip to be wary of. There are also dangerous currents at the N end of the beach, by the mouth of the river Don.

Access   Town Beach is to the north of the city, with plenty of parking above the beach.

Facilities   Being an oil town, Aberdeen offers everything you're likely to need.

Accommodation   Caravan parks and camp sites at Backhill, Garthdee, and South Loirston. There's a youth hostel in the town, and plenty of B & B's.

19 BALMEDIE
➤ Landranger 38 GR 980180

Surf   A northward extension of the beach at Aberdeen, it has similar beach break waves but there are no groynes. The banks tend to shift and this will affect the quality of the waves. Best on a SE or E swell. NW winds are offshore. OK for beginners. There can be a strong longshore drift, usually to the S.

Access   Take the turn-off from the A92 at Balmedie. There's a car park and picnic site above the beach from where you walk through the dunes to the break.

Facilities   There's a shop in the village.

Accommodation   See Newburgh.

20 NEWBURGH
➤ Landranger 38 GR 006236

Surf   There's a right-hander breaking off the mouth of the river Ythan, which is often fast and hollow. Watch out for currents heading out to sea on an outgoing tide or after heavy rains. NW winds are offshore. Not an ideal wave for beginners.

Access   Newburgh is at the junction of the A975 coast road and the B9000 from inland. Park by the golf course at the estuary and walk down to the break.

Facilities   Limited facilities in Newburgh, otherwise the nearest are at Ellon.

Accommodation   There's a caravan park and camp site in Newburgh, otherwise try Aberdeen.

21 CRUDEN BAY
➤ Landranger 30 GR 090350

Surf   A quality beach break with peaks along the length of the two-mile stretch of beach. There's a particularly good peak at the N end of the bay among the salmon nets. Works best on SE or E swells, or big N swells. W to NW winds are offshore. There's a strong rip - beginners should treat this with caution.

Access   The village of Cruden is on the A975. From the car park there's a path across the dunes to the beach.

Facilities   Cafe and shops in the village.

Accommodation   Very little locally.

Long grinding left on Scotland's far north east coast

22 SANDFORD BAY
➤ Landranger 30 GR 124438

Surf   Big N swells wrap into Sandford Bay giving good lefts over a boulder reef on the N side of the bay. W to NW winds are offshore. Not a beginners break.

Access   Take the turn-off from the A952 at the roundabout S of Invernettie to the bay. The road runs above the beach.

Facilities   None at the beach, limited locally, but there are plenty of pubs, shops, and cafes in nearby Peterhead.

Accommodation   Caravan park and camp site in Peterhead.

23 ST COMBS
➤ Landranger 30 GR 058634

Surf   Around St Combs you come to a stretch of coastline that faces NE, then N as you round the corner to Fraserburgh. The surf tends to be bigger here and more consistent than that further south because the coast faces the direction of the most frequent and powerful swells in the North Sea -

those from the N and NE. There are a number of breaks around St Combs - beach breaks to the N and S of the town, and both left and right-hand reefs to the S. These work best around mid tide, and on N or NE swells. SW winds are offshore. The reefs are not suitable for beginners.

Access The B9033 runs through St Combs, from where there's a road down to the beach.

Facilities Limited facilities in St Combs, but shops, cafes and pubs just up the coast at Fraserburgh.

Accommodation Caravan parks and camp sites in Fraserburgh.

24 FRASERBURGH
➤ *Landranger 30 - GRs for individual beaches below*

Surf There are three breaks in and around Fraserburgh, which is generally regarded as the surf centre of NE Scotland:
  1. PHILORTH (GR 020651) The E end of Fraserburgh beach, it's a beach break with a number of peaks dependent on the constantly shifting sand banks. It tends to be bigger and better than the breaks at the W end of the beach. Best just before and after high tide. S to SW winds are offshore. OK for beginners.
  2. THE BROCH (GR 001664) The town end of the beach, this is a beach break working best from mid to high tide. S to SW winds are offshore. OK for beginners. There's also a left over rocks at high tide which is best left to experienced surfers.
  3. THE HARBOUR At the end of the beach is a wave by the harbour wall, which works only on swells over 8ft. There's a left and right here. It's rarely surfed, and usually only works in winter. A wave for experienced surfers only.

Access Philorth is reached from the B9033 running S from Fraserburgh. Turn off into the dunes, where there's ample parking, and walk over the dunes to the beach.
  The other two breaks are in Fraserburgh itself with a car park above them.

Facilities There are toilets, showers, and a changing area above the beach. There's a cafe and shop here plus more shops and pubs in the town. There is a local surf club here, The Broch.

Accommodation There's a caravan park and camp site above the beach in the town and similar facilities

in Fraserbrough and Rosehearty. The scenery consists of huge cliffs, small sandy bays, and picturesque fishing villages. There are excellent views across the Moray Firth (which has one of only two resident dolphin populations in the UK) to the coast and hills of Sutherland and Caithness.

25 PHINGASK SHORE
➤ *Landranger 30, GR 984675*

Surf Just to the W of Fraserburgh. This is a fast, heavy reef break, breaking both left and right. It's best at high tide and picks up swells from any N'ly direction. Long paddle out. S winds are offshore. Only suitable for experienced surfers.

Access Take the B9031 a short way W out of Fraserburgh - you'll really need an OS map to locate the break - and park at the roadside.

Facilities Shops, cafes and pubs in Fraserburgh.

Accommodation See Fraserburgh.

26 SANDHAVEN
➤ *Landranger 30, GR 965676*

Surf West of Phingask, this is another reef break. It has hollow, gnarly lefts and rights breaking in very shallow, rocky water, producing a wave that is not for the inexperienced or faint of heart. It works from mid to three-quarter tide on swells from any N'ly direction. S'ly winds are offshore.

Access Follow the B9031 W out of Fraserburgh and park in front of the break - an OS map or local help will make it a lot easier to find.

Facilities and accommodation See Fraserburgh.

27 BANFF RIVERMOUTH
➤ *Landranger 29 GR 695640*

Surf A beach break at the mouth of the river with lefts and rights breaking into the estuary. Best from mid to high tide. S winds are offshore. Beginners should be wary of rips near the rivermouth on outgoing tides and after heavy rains.

Access The A98 coast road runs through Banff and past the break. Park above the break.

Facilities Shops, cafes and pubs in the town.

Accommodation   There are caravan parks and camp sites in Banff and in the surrounding area.

28 BOYNDIE BAY, BANFF
▶ *Landranger 29 GR 675646*

Surf   An excellent right-hand point break which is best at high tide although it also works from mid tide towards high water. There's also a good left on the other side of the point at low tide and peaks on the beach. Best on a N swell. S'ly winds are offshore. Boyndie Bay is the best quality wave in the area and will hold up to 12ft or so. The beach breaks are fine for beginners on smaller swells.

Access   Boyndie Bay is on the west side of town with roads leading directly to it. There's parking above the beach.

Facilities and accommodation   See Banff Rivermouth.

29 SANDEND BAY
▶ *Landranger 29 GR 554662*

Surf   An attractive little beach with peaks along its length plus a left off the harbour wall at the W end. Best from mid to high tide. S winds are offshore. OK for beginners.

Access   The A98 runs through the village and above the beach. There's a car park within easy reach of the beach.

Facilities   Small shop and restaurant in the village. Toilets in the village.

Accomodation   Caravan parks and camp sites at Sandend, Portsoy and Cullen.

30 CULLEN BAY
▶ *Landranger 29 GR 500677*

Surf   A number of beach breaks along the length of the bay. It faces NE so picks up swells from that direction as well as from the N. Usually neither Cullen nor Sandend are as good as Banff. SW winds are offshore. OK for beginners but be aware of longshore currents.

Access   The A98 runs into the town. There's access to the beach from the golf course and from Seatown. Car park near the harbour.

Facilities   Cafe and hotel in Seatown. Toilets at the harbour. If it's flat you can take sea fishing and boat trips from the harbour.There are bowling greens, tennis courts, putting and a golf course.

Accommodation   See Sandend Bay .

31 LOSSIEMOUTH
▶ *Landranger 28 GR 280680*

Surf   A long, sweeping sandy beach facing NE, with peaks all the way along. It works on all stages of the tide. It picks up NE swells in particular but good N swells too. SW winds are offshore. OK for beginners, but keep an eye open for longshore currents.

Access   The A941 and the B9103 run into Lossiemouth. Don't go right into the town but head for the forest just to the S, from where tracks lead down to the beach. Keep away from the E end of the beach where there is a rifle range.

Facilities   None - the nearest are in the town.

Accommodation   Caravan park and camp site in Lossiemouth. More around Elgin, a few miles inland.

32 ACKERGILL / SINCLAIR'S BAY
▶ *Landranger 12, GR 345555*

Surf   Ackergill is at the S end of Sinclair's Bay. It has two right-hand point breaks, which break onto rocks at the end of the wave - be careful! Best at high tide on a N or NE swell. S to SW winds are offshore. Not a beginner's wave. To the N of Ackergill, Sinclair's Bay curves away for four miles with beach breaks all along. The N end may pick up big SE swells. As you move N up the bay winds from the W then NW become offshore. The beach breaks are OK for beginners. Porpoises and seals can often be seen in the bay.

Access   Go down a road off the A9 to the N of Wick Airfield. Park above the beach next to the golf club.
     Apart from at Keiss at the north end, where there is a car park next to a golf course, access to the rest of Sinclair's Bay is restricted.

Facilities   None.

Accommodation   There are caravan parks and

camp sites at Wick, Nybster, and around John o'Groats, where there's also a youth hostel.

33 SKIRZA HARBOUR / FRESWICK BAY
➤ *Landranger 12, GR 388680*

Surf There are excellent lefts breaking over a boulder reef at the N end of this SE-facing beach. Although it can be surfed all the way through the tides, it's at its best from mid to high water as lots of rocks are exposed at low tide. Works on a SE swell or a big N swell. NW winds are offshore. Not a wave for inexperienced surfers.

Access There's a turn-off from the A9 for Skirza. Park in front of the house overlooking the small harbour - this is private property so ask permission first.

Facilities and Accommodation See Sinclair's Bay.

THE NORTH COAST

The north coast of Scotland is to Britain what the north coast of Maui is to Hawaii. Unfortunately, swaying palm trees, hot sun and blue skies are not a noticeable feature of Britain's 'north shore'. Nevertheless, here is possibly the best chance you have of finding world -class surf in the British Isles. Thurso is the spot that everyone heads for. It's a good base, but there are plenty of quality waves either side of Thurso. There are also plenty of beach breaks that are less daunting than the often big and powerful reef breaks to be found at spots such as Thurso East and Brimms Ness - in effect, something for everyone. The coastline and mountains inland are superb and well worth exploring if there are no waves.

Bear in mind that many of the breaks on the north coast are isolated (so a good map is essential). You can be miles from the nearest town, so if you get into trouble you're on your own. However, there's no reason why that should be a problem if you use your head and remember a couple of the basic rules of surfing - don't go out unless you're sure you can handle the conditions and don't let yourself get too cold in the water.

1 GILLS
➤ *Landranger 12, GR 330729*

Surf A left-hand reef break over a flat rock shelf which may well be worth checking out as an alternative to the more frequently surfed breaks to the W. SW winds are offshore. Be careful if you choose to surf here as there can be very powerful rips from the strong tidal flow through the Pentland Firth where the North Sea and the Atlantic meet. Tidal streams may exceed 10 knots on spring tides. A break for experienced surfers only.

Access Gills is on the A836 coast road. Park at the coast.

Facilities None. The nearest are at Thurso.

Accommodation Caravan parks and camp sites around John o'Groats. Youth hostel. Also see Thurso.

2 SKARFSKERRY
➤ *Landranger 12, GR 270745*

Surf There is a selection of right and left-hand reef breaks here, breaking over flat tongues of rock projecting out to sea. Worth checking. S winds are offshore. Not waves for inexperienced surfers.

Access Take the B855 N from the A836 to the village and park at the coast.

Facilities None - shop and hotel in Dunnet village, otherwise see Thurso.

Accommodation Caravan park and camp site at Dunnet Bay. Also see Gills and Thurso.

3 POINT OF NESS
➤ *Landranger 12, GR 209710*

Surf A long right-hand point break at the N end of Dunnet Bay, breaking in front of the small pier. It can provide very long rides on a big swell, but is rather fickle. Best at high tide. It works on a W or NW swell, and is offshore in winds from the east. Well protected from N winds by Dunnet Head. Beginners would be better sticking to the main beach (see Dunnet Bay).

Access Turn off the A836 at Dunnet and take the minor road into the village, from where you have to walk up to the point.

Facilities   Shop and hotel in Dunnett. Also see
Thurso.

Accommodation   Camp site at Dunnet Bay,
otherwise see Thurso.

4 DUNNET BAY
➤ *Landranger 12, GR 210690*

Surf   A superb sweep of sand backed by impressive
dunes, with beach breaks all along its length. It
works at its best on a NW swell with offshore and
cross-shore winds at an angle to the beach, otherwise
it tends to close out, so look for winds from S to E.
A good beach for beginners, although there are rips
to watch out for at the S end. There are quicksands
on either side of the stream - the dangerous area is
indicated by notices.

Access   The A836 runs alongside the beach, with
parking just off the road at either end of the bay.

Facilities   Shop and hotel in Dunnett, otherwise see
Thurso. The area is a nature reserve, and the ranger,
based in the main car park, will provide guided
walks along the shore and through the forest behind
the dunes.

Accommodation   Camp site by the beach,
otherwise see Thurso.

5 MURKLE / CASTLETOWN AREA

Surf   There are four breaks in the area:
   1. NOTHING LEFT - A left-hand reef break
along the coast from Murkle towards Castletown.
It's a ridiculously fast wave, and if you make it to the
end you'll discover why it is so named.
   2. SILAS CORNER - Another left-hand reef
break inside Nothing Left, also extremely fast.
   3. THE PEAK - As the name implies, a peak
breaking over rocks out at sea, with a fast left-
hander. Steep, fast take-off.
   All three breaks are best from mid to high tide on
a NW to N swell.
   4. THE SPUR - A left-hand point break which
wraps around the headland into Murkle Bay, and
has a fast bowling section on the inside. It's best at
mid tide. When it's working it can be seen from the
road. It's rarely surfed though, and is a hazardous
spot, so don't go out here alone.
   Grid references have been omitted from this
section, because the only sure-fire way of finding the
breaks is to ask the local surfers.

Access   Murkle is a short way off the A836 on a
minor road. Park in the village and walk to the
breaks.

Facilities and Accommodation   See Dunnet Bay
and/or Thurso (Murkle is more or less mid way
between the two).

6 THURSO EAST (CASTLE REEF)
➤ *Landranger 12, GR 125691*

Surf   Few people would dispute the fact that
Thurso East is one of the best waves in Europe. A
right-hand reef break over a flat, kelp-covered rock
shelf made up of Thurso flagstone, it's best on a big
NW swell. It really begins to show its class when it
gets over 8ft, and it can hold surfable waves of 12-15
ft and up. High tide is usually best, especially on a
big swell, when it's a fast, barreling, go-for-it wave.
Tube rides are the order of the day at Thurso East
and are often the only way of making the wave. As
the tide drops, the wave tends to get slower, and, on
small swells, it can drag on the kelp. S to SE winds
are offshore.
   This is definitely not a wave for beginners.
Surfers of little experience may find it better to wait
for the tide to drop when the wave becomes a little
less formidable.
   On a good swell, this is the one spot on the north
coast that's likely to be crowded for Thurso has the
largest population of surfers in Scotland.

Access   Take the dirt track towards the castle off the
A836 on the E side of Thurso. Follow this to the
end and park above the break in the surfers carpark.

Facilities   None at the break itself, but Thurso is
the largest town on the N coast and has shops,
supermarkets, cafes and pubs. It also has a surf shop
(see Appendix). There is a ferry to the Shetland and
Orkney Isles - take your board, you may find waves
in the Orkneys.

Accommodation   There are two caravan parks and
camp sites in Thurso. Hotels in the town.

7 THURSO REEF
➤ *Landranger 12, GR 120690*

Surf   This is a left and right hand reef break which
can, on occasion, produce an excellent wave in front
of the harbour wall. It will never be as big or as
hollow as Thurso East, although it can hold waves
up to around 8ft. It works all the way through the

tide, but is better from low to medium S to SW winds which are offshore. This is the site of the town's main sewage outfall. Pollution shouldn't be too bad, though, because it is piped a mile out to sea. Suitable for less experienced surfers.

Access Take the road down to the harbour from the centre of Thurso, and park above the break in the pier carpark.

Facilities and Accommodation See Thurso East .

8 THURSO BEACH
➤ *Landranger 12, GR 115687*

Surf The two reefs will almost always be better than the beach, but when the latter is working it can produce very good left and right-hand peaks, although it often lacks good banks. It provides an alternative to the reefs for beginners and inexperienced surfers. It's better from low to three-quarter tide, as backwash at high tide spoils the waves. SW winds are offshore.

Access Parking space is usually available close to the beach.

Facilities and accommodation See Thurso East.

9 BRIMMS NESS GRAVEYARD
➤ *Landranger 12, GR 04071*

Surf (see diagram) This is the spot to head for if everywhere else is flat. Brimms Ness consists of a series of flat flagstone ledges, which catch swell from any direction, and particularly the west. It can be a good 4ft here when there's nothing at Thurso. Don't be deceived by what you see from the main road above the break as this is some 2 miles away. If you can see anything at all that resembles surf there will almost certainly be useful waves here. The name Graveyard comes from the graveyard above the breaks and not the result of the frequent bone crunching wipeouts that occur here!

There are three breaks here, all reefs:

1. THE POINT - A left-hander, which holds waves up to around 20ft, although at this size it would need an extremely good surfer or a madman to go out in it. There's a lot of water moving about and some bad rips on a big swell. It really isn't advisable to attempt The Point once it gets above 10-12ft. This is a low tide wave, breaking over a shallow rock ledge. As with the other two breaks at

Thurso East, one of Europe's premier reef breaks

Brimms, winds from the S are offshore.

2. THE COVE - A short, fast, hollow right-hander, working up to about 8ft. Best at low tide. Breaks in very shallow water - a wipeout here can give both ego and body a serious battering.

3. THE BOWL - Another short right-hander breaking in very shallow water: extremely hollow and fast. It works up to about 8ft (at which point there's a good chance there'll be waves at Thurso). Mid to high tide is best. Hollowest on very high tides.

None of these waves are in any way suitable for beginners or inexperienced surfers, and none of them hold a crowd. A helmet is well worthwhile when surfing here.

Access You take a turn-off to the coast from the A836 some three miles W of Thurso, and follow a narrow lane for two miles that finishes at a farm above the break. The farmer has built a carpark for especially for surfers so please respect his property.

Facilities and Accommodation None, see Thurso.

10 SANDSIDE BAY
➤ *Landranger 11, GR 960655*

Surf There are two good left-hand reef breaks by the harbour, and a low tide peak on the beach, with a left and a better right. The reefs are best from mid to high tide. It gets very shallow at low water. Big swells may join together to give a long ride all the way to the beach. There's a tendency for the break furthest from the harbour to back off on high tide. Winds from S are offshore. The reefs are not suitable for beginners. Although not as powerful as Brimms Ness or Thurso, Sandside is a good option if the latter are too big.

Access Sandside is situated just W of Dounreay nuclear power station. I've been told by Greenpeace that there are serious concerns over the level of radioactivity in the seas around Sandside and Brimms Ness. To get there, turn off the A836 to the bay and park by the beach or harbour.

Facilities None locally, see Thurso.

Accommodation Caravan park and camp site at nearby Reay.

11 MELVICH
➤ *Landranger 10, GR 880650*

Surf Melvich has peaks all over the beach on shifting sand banks, and good lefts and rights breaking off a boulder reef by the river mouth.

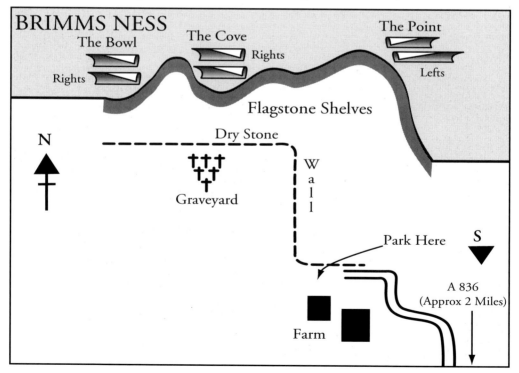

There's also a right-hander at the river mouth at low tide. The rest of the breaks work at all stages of the tide and are generally better on a N swell. Melvich will only hold waves up to about 6ft. The boulder reef tends to have better waves after heavy rains have washed silt from the river on to the reef. The river provides an easy paddle out, but look out for strong currents running out to sea after heavy rains. S to SW winds are offshore. Reasonably safe for beginners.

Access   A single track road leads off the A836 to the bay. Drive into 'private' road, turn left and park in the carpark by bridge. West of Melvich the A836 becomes a single track road with passing places.

Facilities   Hotel and post office at Portskerra to the W of the bay.

Accommodation   Other than the hotel, nothing locally.

12 STRATHY
➤ *Landranger 10, GR 835660*

Surf   A pleasant bay with beach breaks along its length, working at all stages of the tide. As with all the beach breaks W of Thurso, Strathy requires a

bigger swell to work than is required by the reefs around Thurso. The river mouth is also worth checking for a wave. S winds are offshore, although the high cliffs at the W end of the bay provide shelter from W winds. OK for beginners.

Access   Down a single track road through sand dunes from the A836.

Facilities   Inn and post office in the village.

Accommodation   Nearest camp site is in Bettyhill.

13 ARMADALE
➤ *Landranger 10, GR 795647*

Surf   A small bay facing NNW, with beach breaks at low tide. Better on NW and N swells. Winds from S are offshore. OK for beginners.

Access   A side road off the A836 goes into Armadale. Park to the W of the bay.

Neil Harries, The Bowl, Brimms Ness

Facilities   Hotel and Post Office in village.

Accommodation   Nearest camp site is at Bettyhill.

14 FARR BAY
➤ *Landranger 10, GR 714626*

Surf   A small bay with beach breaks that tend to be more consistent than those on surrounding beaches. Faces NW and is quite well open to swells from this direction. Works at all stages of the tide. SE winds are offshore. OK for beginners.

Access   Just off the A836 - visible from the road. Park above the beach.

Facilities   Shops, pub, and tourist information in nearby Bettyhill.

Accommodation   Camp site in Bettyhill.

15 TORRISDALE
➤ *Landranger 10, GR 695620*

Surf   An excellent right-hand river mouth break over a sand bottom, fast and long, and rarely surfed. I've heard it compared to Kirra, Burleigh, and Padang Padang! I haven't seen it working for myself so can't comment, but any wave with those credentials has got to be worth checking if there's a swell.

The wave breaks off the rivermouth at the E end of this superb bay and has a number of hollow sections - you've got to get tubed to make them, but if you do you'll have a long, long ride that will leave your legs like jelly at the end. The bay faces NNW, and is offshore in S to SW winds. It works well in SW gales. Needs a big swell to work, breaking when Thurso East gets over 6ft. You have to paddle out to the break from the rivermouth - watch out for rips on a big swell or after heavy rains. Not a beginner's wave.

There are beach breaks along the beach too, and a rivermouth break at the W end of the bay, but it entails a long drive around the estuary of the river (or a long walk along the beach) to reach it.

Access   Through Bettyhill to the N, and the road comes out above the mouth of the river after about 1/2 mile. Walk down to the river and paddle out. You can reach the W end of the beach from the village of Torrisdale.

Facilities   Limited shops, pub, in Bettyhill.

Accommodation   Camp site at Bettyhill.

There are waves around the mouth of the Kyle of Tongue at Coldbackie, and Rabbit Island. The beaches face NW to N, and are blocked to a large extent by headlands and islands. On a large swell, when all the other beaches are closed out, this area may well be worth a visit.

You should take care when surfing here, as there can be dangerous currents from the Kyle water emptying into the sea on an outgoing tide. The area is pretty isolated so you're likely to be on your own. I don't have any more detailed information, but if you want to explore there's plenty of potential.

16 DURNESS AREA

This is the main town on the NW coast, and it's surrounded by impressive scenery. The beaches are clean white or golden sands, extremely quiet, and washed by crystal clear waters. Behind them rise the impressive peaks of Ben Hope, Cranstackie, and Foinaven.

In the town there are a couple of reasonably well-stocked shops, garages, a pub with a great view over Sango Bay, and a good camp site well-situated next to the beach. There's also a youth hostel. The tourist information people (next to the pub. Tel: 01971 511259) are very helpful and keen to promote surfing in the area.

CEANNABEINNE (Landranger 9 GR 443657) - A NE-facing beach which is a better bet than SANGOBEG BAY, just to the NW which is blocked from most swells by offshore islands. Best at high tide. There are peaks along the length of the beach, which at low tide joins Traigh na h-Uamhag. SW winds offshore. Parking above beach. No other facilities.

SANGO BAY (Landranger 9 GR 408677) - In the centre of Durness and well situated for all the facilities the town has to offer. There are peaks all along the beach, rights and lefts off the rock in the middle of the beach, and a right-hander off the cliffs at the SE end of the bay. Picks up NE and N swells and big NW swells. On a good swell it works at all stages of the tide, otherwise best at high tide. SW winds are offshore. OK for beginners. Plenty of parking above the beach.

BALNAKIEL BAY (Landranger 9 GR 393690) - A W-facing beach, well placed to pick up swells from the west and also bigger N swells. Beach breaks along its length which work at all stages of the tide. Winds from NE to SE are offshore. OK for beginners.

THE WEST COAST

The west coast of Scotland - including the islands - has some of the most impressive coastal scenery in Europe - some would say the world. The amount of surf on the mainland is limited as the coast is sheltered by the Western Isles. However, the more westerly of the islands pick up any swell going, and have tremendous potential for good waves. Few of them are surfed regularly, and it's quite possible that a visit to one of the less frequented islands could find you being the first person ever to surf certain breaks. Crowds will certainly be the least of your worries.

The seas off the west coast are noticeably warmer than the north and east of Scotland, being washed by the 'warm' North Atlantic Drift. They're also, on the whole, very clean.

The big drawback to the west coast is the difficulty of access. Few of the mainland breaks are easily reached and travelling out to the islands is a major - and expensive - surfari.

Facilities of any sort, from shops to camp sites, are often sparse, and there are no surf shops.

THE MAINLAND

1 SANDWOOD BAY
➤ *Landranger 9 GR 220655*

Surf One of the most remote and scenic beaches in Britain, this really is the Scottish coast at its best. This exposed beach faces NW and will pick up any swell going. There are peaks all along its length, plus waves off the rocks in the middle of the beach, and a break at the river mouth (this has now shifted and is at the NE end of the beach and not as marked on the OS map). Beware of rips near the rocks.

The beach breaks work at all stages of the tide, and the river mouth at low water: from mid tide it tends to back off and there's also backwash off the cliffs. Winds from south through to east are offshore.

As is the case with many of the beaches on the NW and W coast, their isolation makes them unsuitable for learners, and even experienced surfers would be well advised to check the breaks thoroughly from the beach for rips, especially on big swells. ALWAYS surf with a friend. If you get into trouble at a break like Sandwood Bay you really are on your own.

Access Take the B801 to Kinlochbervie off the

A838 coast road. From here head to Oldshoremore then Blairmore, just after which there's a turn-off down a dirt track to Sandwood Bay.

If you value your suspension, you can park at the start of the track and walk the full four miles to the beach. Alternatively, bump your way down the first couple of miles until the track becomes impassable and tackle the rest on foot. Either way, just pray there's a wave waiting when you get there!

Facilities None - apart from the scenery. The beach is virtually untouched by man. Golden sands with a lagoon and loch behind them are backed by a pass up into the moors and mountains of Sutherland. The beach is hemmed in at either end by impressive cliffs and a stack at the SW end. If it's solitude your after, this is the place to head for - it would be a great place to camp in good weather (but beware of the midges).

Accommodation Caravan park and camp sites in Balchrick and Oldshoremore.

2 POLIN BEACH
➤ *Landranger 9 GR 190590*

Surf A small SW facing beach with peaks at all stages of the tide. There are rights off the cliffs at the NW end. NE winds are offshore. OK for beginners.

Access Take the road from Oldshoremore (see Sandwood Bay) to Oldshore Beg, where you can park above the beach and walk through a field down to it.

Facilities Basic groceries, and post office in Oldshoremore.

Accommodation See Sandwood Bay.

3 OLDSHOREMORE
➤ *Landranger 9 GR 198587*

Surf A beach break similar to Polin. Peaks at all stages of the tide, but needs a big swell to work. There are also good waves off a rocky outcrop in the middle of the beach. NE winds are offshore. OK for beginners.

Access Park above the beach by Oldshoremore cemetery and walk down.

Facilities and Accommodation See Polin and Sandwood Bay.

Scotland's mainland west coast between here and the Kintyre peninsula has little or no surf due to the various islands, blocking the swells.

MULL OF KINTYRE

4 BELLOCHANTUY BAY,
➤ *Landranger 68, GR 663325*

Surf   The waves here break over a sand bar which has a tendency to shift taking the peaks with it. It's best on a rising tide with a W'ly swell. E'ly winds are offshore. OK for beginners provided that the swell isn't too big.

Access   About 11 miles NW of Campbelltown along the A83, the main road down the peninsula. Park above the beach.

Facilities   Hotel in village. Also see Machrihanish.

Accommodation   Caravan park and camp site at Dalkeith. Also see Machrihanish.

5 WESTPORT / THE GRAVEYARD
➤ *Landranger 68, GR 655263*

Surf   At the N end of Machrihanish Bay, and overlooked by a graveyard - hence the name. This is a beach break over a sand bar about 200 yards out to sea, which is best surfed on a rising tide. Needs a W'ly swell and tends to pick up more swell than other beaches. The rights tend to be better, and it can hold good-sized waves - up to around 12 feet. E'ly winds are offshore. Watch out for rips, especially on larger swells.

Access   From the A83, where there's parking above the beach.

Facilities   None - see Machrihanish.

Accommodation   None - see Machrihanish.

6 MACHRIHANISH BAY

Surf   A four mile long bay with the village of Machrihanish at the S end and Westport at the N end. There are beach breaks all along the bay which faces N at the southern end then curves round to face W for the rest of its length. There are good lefts

and rights to be had, better from low tide up,(although there's only a 4-6ft difference between low and high tide) with the peaks tending to shift as the sand banks are moved about. Best on a W'ly swell. Winds from S through to E are offshore depending which part of the beach you're on. There are rips at high tide.

Recently the middle of the bay has been more regularly surfed, as it tends to have the best peaks.

It can hold good-sized waves and is becoming increasingly popular with boardsailers who regularly hold contests here.

Access   You can reach the N end from Westport. For the middle, go through the RAF base to a farm gate, go through the gate, turn left after 100 yds, then drive half a mile along a track to the dunes. The B843 from Campbelltown leads to the S end of the beach, where you can park.

Facilities   None at the beach. The Beachcomber Inn in Machrihanish is worth a visit. The only comprehensive facilities in the area are in Campbelltown, six miles E.

Accommodation   Caravan park and camp site in Machrihanish.

7 CARSKIEY BAY
➤ *Landranger 68, GR 660077*

Surf   A south-facing beach with a low tide reef break, and left and right-hand beach breaks that work all through the tide. Picks up surf when it's too big or blown out on the W coast, of from S swells coming up the Irish Sea. Unfortunately, it doesn't work very often. N to NW winds are offshore. The reef is not suitable for beginners.

Access   Take the B842 to Southend from Campbelltown, then due W for about a mile to Carskiey village. Park above beach.

Facilities   None at the beach. Pub in Southend, otherwise try Campbelltown.

Accommodation   Very little locally, see Machrihanish.

8 DUNAVERTY BAY
➤ *Landranger 68, GR 685078*

Surf   A SW-facing beach with beach breaks and a

fast right off the rocks at the W end of the beach. This is best from mid tide up. Best on a big W swell or on a S swell coming up the Irish Sea. N to NW winds are offshore. OK for beginners, but keep away from the rocks at either end of the beach.

Access Take the B842 into Southend - the road runs S to the beach. Park above the beach.

Facilities and Accommodation See Carskeiy Bay.

THE HEBRIDES

The Inner and Outer Hebrides are great places in which to surf - each island is different; each has its own character and atmosphere, but all share remote, wild, unspoilt landscapes, clear green seas, and, at times, excellent quality surf.

The climate is very unpredictable. Periods of rain and wind can occur at any time of year.

Because the islands are so infrequently surfed, I have only limited information on the surf to be found there despite having surfed there myself.

The remote nature of the beaches, and the potential size and power of the waves, mean the islands are not really ideally suited to inexperienced surfers.

There's often only one main road on any particular island, with a number of smaller, but often pretty rough, minor roads to beaches. In some cases you won't be able to reach some stretches of coast by road if you decide to explore. Many of the road signs are in Gaelic - which is used more often here than on the mainland - and may take a bit of getting used to. There are absolutely no surf shops - in fact shops of any kind are often few and far between. Everything closes on a Sunday.

All the islands can be reached by Caledonian MacBrayne ferry from the mainland. For details of the various routes and prices contact Caledonian MacBrayne, The Ferry Terminal, Gouroch PA19 1QP (01475 33755). They have special Rover tickets which allow unlimited travel over one or two weeks for a set price.

THE OUTER HEBRIDES - LEWIS

A rocky, barren, and often windswept island, dotted with tiny lochs, and ancient burial chambers and standing stones. There's little activity, and few people, outside the capital of Stornoway. Trees are few and far between.

Stornoway itself is surprisingly lively considering its distance from the mainland and it has all major facilities and the locals are very friendly. It's the main point of access to the mainland, with a car ferry to Ullapool. Camping is limited to a camp site in Stornoway, and one or two other caravan parks and camp sites dotted here and there on the island. You should be able to camp above many of the beaches without offending anybody. There are a number of holiday cottages in the area and B&B's. Of all the islands off the west coast, Lewis is the most exposed to swells - if there's any action at all in the North Atlantic, the chances are that Lewis will get it. The beaches here are fantastic - clear green-blue seas and golden sands backed by dunes.

1 BARVAS
➤ *Landranger 8, GR 343512*

Surf A pebble beach with a number of very exposed boulder reefs which catch any swells and can often be over 10ft. There are both rights and lefts here. SE winds are offshore. Don't get swept out to sea - the next stop is Newfoundland!

Access Take the turn-off to Lower Barvas at the junction of the A858 and A857. A bumpy dirt track takes you past a football pitch to the beach.

Facilities None.

Accommodation Local B&B.

2 DALMORE BAY
➤ *Landranger 8, GR 215451*

Surf More exposed and usually a couple of feet bigger than Valtos to the S. There's a good peak over a sandbar at the N end of the beach. Watch out for a very bad rip along the cliffs at the S end - if you lose your board here you could be in real trouble. S winds are offshore.

Access A minor road off the A858 at Upper Carloway leads to the beach, which is overlooked by two graveyards (a common feature of many Scottish beaches).

Facilities None other than public toilets.

Accommodation None.

3 VALTOS
➤ *Landranger 13, GR 085365*

Surf A beach break which is highly rated. It catches swells through from NW to bigger S swells. It's quite well sheltered, with winds from the south being offshore.

Access There's a turn off to Valtos from the B8011. Park above the beach.

Facilities None. It was brought to my notice that the non-surfing locals might not be too pleased if you surf here on a Sunday as the church overlooks the beach. At least take a Bible out with you.

Accommodation Caravan site at Kneep, just to the east.

4 MANGERSTA SANDS
➤ *Landranger 13, GR 008308*

Surf I have it on good authority that a group of very experienced surfers pronounced this area too dangerous to surf, but conditions may not always be so critical. I leave it up to you to decide for yourself.

Access Take the B8011 to Uig Sands, from where Mangersta is a couple of miles S.

Facilities and Accommodation None.

A few more spots worth checking out include Eoropie (at the Butt of Lewis), Bragar (to the SW of Eoropie) and Rhuba Phail, a beach break holding big waves to the south of Uig Sands.

HARRIS

Harris has some beautiful beaches, especially the huge crescent of Traigh Scarasta in the SW. With the exception of this beach, Harris isn't as exposed to swells as Lewis. However, the beaches along the NE coast are all close together, and may repay a visit. There's a small camp site at Seilebost at the N end of this stretch of coastline. Other than this, accommodation and shops are few and far between outside the main town of Tarbert. From Tarbert you can catch the ferry to Lochmaddy, on North Uist, and to the mainland.

NORTH UIST, BENBECULA, AND SOUTH UIST

These three islands are connected by road bridges, and unlike their neighbours to the north, are a little greener and slightly less barren. The traditional occupation of western Scotland, peat digging, is clearly in evidence here, and a few crofters' cottages remain.

The main towns are Lochmaddy (North Uist), which has a youth hostel, a garage, shop, and pub; Balivanich (Benbecula), which has reasonably good shops (including a sports/windsurfing shop), and Lochboisdale (South Uist), which also has limited facilities. A ferry runs from Lochboisdale to the mainland. There's a caravan park at Borve on South

Checking out the North Shore juice, Brimms Ness

Uist and campsites at Liniclate, Benbecula and Borve.

I was unlucky and didn't see any waves while I was there, but I have it on good authority that there are reef, point and beach breaks to be found all down the west coast of the islands. Here are a couple that have potential.

1. Scrifearnach, North Uist - An impressive crescent of sand which faces NW. Offshore winds will vary, depending where you are on the beach. There's a rivermouth at the S end which would probably have waves. You can drive all the way to the beach from the minor road out of Sollas by the Co-op store.

2. Culla Bay, Benbecula - A small bay which did have a wave when I visited but it was small, onshore, and of poor quality; but it looked as though it might hold surfable waves in both onshore and offshore winds.

South Uist has long stretches of beach facing directly W, interspersed with a number of points which show potential reef breaks such as Rhuba Ardvule Point. When checking them out watch out for nesting Arctic terns - they will dive bomb you and peck you on the head to try to get you away from their nests.

THE INNER HEBRIDES

Not quite so exposed to Atlantic swells as the Outer Hebrides, the Inner Hebrides, are, as their name suggests, nearer the mainland, but still pick up plenty of swell. Ferry fares to these islands are slightly cheaper.

TIREE

Reached by car ferry from Oban on the mainland, Because of the strong winds that prevail, Tiree is more popular with boardsailors than surfers. It's also small, very flat, and barren, so there's little protection from the wind.

There are beaches all around Tiree exposed to swells from N, S, and W, so the chances are that if there are waves you'll be able to find somewhere that's offshore. Beaches worth checking are: Balephetrish, The Hough, The Maze (popular with boardsailors, it's a good beach and point break), Port Bharrapol, Balephuil Bay (has good beach breaks).

ISLAY

Islay is less barren than many of the other islands of the Hebrides and it is easily reached from the mainland. There are several small towns and villages which offer all the necessities of life. Islay is famed for its whisky distilleries - there are six on the island and all give guided tours; so there's plenty to occupy your time if it's flat!

There are ferries from Kennacraig on the mainland to Port Askaig and Port Ellen. There's a caravan park and camp site at Laggan Bay, and a camp site at Port Charlotte.

1 SALIGO BAY
➤ *Landranger 60 GR 207665*

Surf A very heavy wave comparable to French beach breaks. There's also a heavy shore break at high tide, and powerful currents. Not a break for inexperienced surfers. E to SE winds are offshore.

Access A minor road off the B8018 leads to dunes above the beach.

Facilities & accommodation None - although you might camp in the dunes.

2 MACHIR BAY
➤ *Landranger 60 GR 207630*

Surf Beach break peaks over sandbars. If Saligo is too big it's usually smaller here. E to NNE winds are offshore.

Access There's a minor road off the B8018 that runs to the beach.

Facilities & Accommodation None - but you might camp in the dunes.

3 LAGGAN BAY

Surf A long sweeping bay which faces W and has an airstrip behind the beach. It works only on bigger swells and has a tendency to close out unless offshore winds are blowing at an angle to it.

Access Just off the A846 road to Bowmore.

Facilities None.

Accommodation Caravan park and camp site at south end of bay.

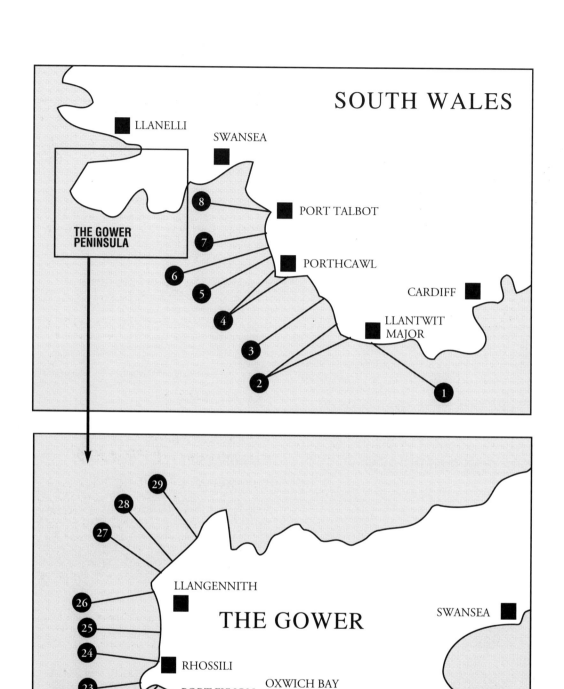

SOUTH WALES

LLANELLI

SWANSEA

PORT TALBOT

PORTHCAWL

CARDIFF

LLANTWIT
MAJOR

THE GOWER
PENINSULA

8
7
6
5
4
3
2
1

THE GOWER

LLANGENNITH

SWANSEA

RHOSSILI

PORT EYNON

OXWICH BAY

MUMBLES
HEAD

29
28
27
26
25
24
23
22
21
20
19
18
17
16
15
14
13
12
11
10
9
8
7
6
5
4
3
2
1

9 SOUTH WALES & THE GOWER PENINSULA

This area is the centre of Welsh surfing. Although relatively neglected by the media when compared with Cornwall, the standard of surfing here is every bit as high. There's an enormous variety of waves in the area, from mellow beach breaks, ideal for beginners, to gnarly reef breaks.

At present much of the area is seriously under threat from pollution, and many surfers have suffered from sore throats, stomach bugs, ear infections etc - directly related to the waste that's pumped into the seas off South Wales. Even Welsh Water and the National River Authority have admitted that there's much room for improvement in the water quality. Increased media coverage has brought the problem out into the open and there's hope that things may start to improve. But you would be well advised not to swallow seawater close to the more industrialised areas.

The Gower peninsula is a relatively unspoilt area of cliffs and coves, beaches and headlands, narrow twisting country roads and small villages.

CLIMATE

The biggest and most consistent swells are to be found in winter, but autumn with its milder air and water temperatures may also be good. Useful waves can occur in spring, but water temperatures will be at their lowest then. In the summer you may expect some reasonable surf interspersed with long periods of pretty flat water.

The climate is very similar to that of Cornwall, perhaps very slightly cooler. Winter air temperatures average 7°C (42°F), rising to about 21°C (70°F) in summer. Water temperatures vary from about 7°C (42°F) in winter to 16°C (60°F) or more in summer.

In winter you'll need a 5/3mm steamer, boots and as it gets colder, gloves and possibly a hood. In summer a 3/2mm steamer should be fine, you may even get away with a spring suit on warmer days.

South Wales and the Gower Peninsula pick up the same swells as Cornwall and Devon, although they tend to be a little smaller here. As a depression moves in from the Atlantic, winds will swing round from S to NW over a period of three to four days and push in a swell. If the depression remains over the Atlantic, then the area may have a combination of excellent surf and fine weather.

South Wales and the Gower have some of the largest tidal ranges in Britain, varying from 9.5 metres (31ft) to just over 13 metres (42.6ft); so reference to a tide table is essential when surfing here. Because of the exceptional tidal range, especially on springs, it always pays to be at a break at the recommended stage of the tide or you may miss the wave.

SOUTH WALES

1 LLANTWIT MAJOR
➤ *Landranger 170, GR 955675*

Surf Probably the best break in the area, this is a right and left-hand peak breaking over a boulder reef known as Col-Huw Point, with the right being the better. It can produce some excellent waves giving long, fast rides, but it needs a big swell to work. It's best from low to mid tide and in calm conditions or in N to E winds. The wave here is usually bigger than it looks, and there can be strong rip currents, so it's not an ideal wave for novices.

Access The B4270 runs in to Llantwit Major from Cowbridge. There's a road to the beach from the town, and car parking above the beach.

Facilities Shops, pubs, etc close by in the town. Lifeguards patrol the beach in summer.

Accommodation Caravan park in Llantwit Major.

2 NASH POINT AREA

I lack information on this stretch of coast, but there are several reef breaks to be found by anyone who can be bothered to explore. A look at the OS map will show that there's plenty of potential for surf along the stretch of coast between Llantwit Major and Southerndown with numerous areas of flat rock slabs projecting out to sea which must get waves.

3 OGMORE-BY-SEA
➤ *Landranger 170, GR 860750*

Surf A SW-facing rivermouth break at the mouth of the Ogmore river that can provide good clean lefts. It's rather fickle and needs a big clean swell to be at its best. It works on an incoming neap tide from mid to high. Best in NE winds, which are offshore. The river can cause strong rips, which make it unsuitable for beginners. Pollution from the river can also be a problem.

Access The B4524 runs through the town, with turn-offs to the beach. There'a a car park above the beach.

Facilities Limited facilities at the beach, shops in the town plus a surf shop (see Appendix). Lifeguards in summer.

Accommodation Caravan park in Ogmore-by-Sea.

From Ogmore east to Southerndown there are a number of breaks, best at low tide, but close to the cliffs, so be careful if surfing here. One such example is BOOBIES, reached by following the Ogmore river road east until you come to a pub on the right. Park here and take the path from the bottom of the car park to the beach. It only works on bigger swells.

Southerndown one mile south of Ogmore, also has waves breaking over a SW-facing sand and pebble beach. Surf from low tide to just before high water. The beach is patrolled by lifeguards in summer.

4 PORTHCAWL

There are several breaks in Porthcawl:
BLACK ROCK/TRECCO BAY - This is the small bay at the eastern end of the town. There's a point break here off Rhych Point (Black Rock) on the west side of the bay. When it's working well it can produce a long, fast right-hander, best at high tide. N to NE winds are offshore. OK for beginners.
CONEY BEACH/SANDY BAY - Immediately west of Black Rock. This is a sandy, south-facing bay which needs a big swell to work, when it can produce a number of peaks from mid to high tide, plus a heavy inside shore break. There may also be a

right-hander off the harbour wall on very low tides. There can be a strong rip along the rocks of Rhych Point which inexperienced surfers should avoid. N to NE winds are offshore.
PORTHCAWL POINT - A south-facing point break which can be fickle, but when working it produces a good hollow right-hander up to about six feet. The waves break over a fairly flat rock shelf. It's easily spoiled by the wind and only works well in N winds. Not recommended for beginners.

To the west of Porthcawl Point there are a couple of small SW-facing bays, sandy at low tide, but nothing but rock at high tide. They produce waves at lower stages of the tide, but you should watch out for the rocks as the tide rises.

Opposite Porthcawl Pier Hotel there's a good left-hander, breaking over rocks; this works best in a NW wind.

Access All the breaks are easily reached from the centre of Porthcawl, which is only about three miles from the M4. This makes it a good stop-off point for surfers travelling further west who fancy breaking their journey for a quick surf. There's plenty of parking close to all the beaches.

Facilities There's a large and very active surf population in and around Porthcawl and when there's a swell running the breaks are likely to be crowded.

Pollution is a problem here - the water is always pretty murky, and the stuff causing the murkiness is not always good for your health.

Shops, cafes and pubs are to be found in abundance at or close to the beaches. There are also surf shops in the town (see Appendix).

For apres-surf entertainment there's plenty of nightlife in the town, and I understand that the Rose and Crown pub is a popular watering hole with local surfers.

Accommodation There are caravan parks and campsites locally.

5 REST BAY
➤ *Landranger 170, GR 820764*

Surf A popular beach break just N of Porthcawl. The waves tend to be rather slow and work at most stages of the tide giving both lefts and rights. A longshore current can be a problem at times, requiring constant paddling to stop you drifting in front of the cliffs. NE winds are offshore. When it's closed out here Black Rock and Coney Beach may be worth checking.

Access There's a road along the coast to Rest Bay from Porthcawl with ample parking above the beach.

Facilities Shops etc. above the bay.

Accommodation See Porthcawl.

6 KENFIG SANDS
► *Landranger 170, GR 790800*

Surf The two and a half miles of sands have a number of beach break peaks which can give long lefts and rights, and are well-suited to beginners on smaller swells. They work at all stages of the tide, with a nice peak in front of the Prince of Wales pub (it's a 20-minute walk from the pub through the dunes to the break). The rocky promontory at the S end of the beach has three bowl-type peaks working from low to mid tide, and at high tide too on big swells. NE winds are offshore.

Access Kenfig is about two miles north of Porthcawl on the coast road. There's a large car park behind the dunes, from where it's quite a trek to the beach.

Facilities Pub by the dunes, also see Porthcawl.

Accommodation Caravan park at Kenfig, also see Porthcawl.

7 MORFA MAWR / MARGAM SANDS
► *Landranger 170, GR 770850*

Surf A long stretch of beach with the idyllic backdrop of the huge British Steel works - the smell is great if the wind's offshore. There are peaks at most stages of the tide along the beach, and a good right-hander off the pier at the N end of the beach, which is sheltered from NW winds which spoil it further south. This hollow wave works at low tide and breaks on a sand bar. NE winds are offshore. The water here can be heavily polluted.

Access These breaks are almost within sight of the M4, and are reached via a private British Steel road at Margam.

Facilities None.

Accommodation None.

ABERAVON
► *Landranger 170, GR 740900*

Surf Aberavon has a beach and a reef break. It's a very popular spot, and is one of the most consistent places in the area, so crowds may be a problem. It is also pretty badly polluted.

The Beach - A left hander, best two hours after low tide and one hour before high water. It picks up more swell than other local breaks and can produce a nice wall and a good long wave when it's working well. NE winds are offshore, but it also works in E winds. NW winds make a mess of it.

The Reef - Located in front of 'Small Warren', this only works on a big SW swell, and gives a nice left into the beach, and a hollow right-hander. It's protected by the pier from most winds other than SE. Not really suitable for novices.

Access Aberavon is only a few minutes drive from the M4 along the B4286. There's a car park above the beach.

Facilities Plenty of shops, pubs and cafes in Aberavon. Lifeguards in summer.

Accommodation See Porthcawl or Gower.

THE GOWER PENINSULA

Gower has a remarkably large and varied number of breaks considering the size of the area. However, this is the focal point of Welsh surfing, so don't expect to get the waves all to yourself.

The area is easily reached from the M4, with a variety of exits available to you depending on which part of the peninsula you're heading for. If you're going to the Mumbles area, it's best to turn off at Junction 46 or 47 (thus avoiding having to drive through Swansea). Take the B4489 from Junction 46 or the A483 from Junction 47 - the route is well signposted.

If you're heading towards the western end of Gower, take the exit at Junction 47, from where there are a number of routes to the Llangennith area. This route is well signposted.

The area's nightlife is pretty good, with a number of busy pubs and clubs along the 'Mumbles mile', and there's usually plenty of action at The King's Head at Llangennith which is popular with surfers.

1 CRAB ISLAND
➤ *Landranger 159, GR 612869*

Surf A right-hand point break just offshore from Langland Bay. It breaks in front of a small rocky islet and is often fast and hollow on the take-off and inside section. It works only two hours either side of low tide, when the islet is exposed. It will hold good sized waves, well over head high, from W or SW swells. It is easily spoilt when it gets windy. NE to WNW winds are offshore. Crab Island is one of the best waves in the area, so it's often crowded when the surf's good and the locals don't suffer fools gladly.

Access Most easily reached from Mumbles via the B4593 off the main A4067 through Mumbles. There's a turn-off from the B4593 down the hill to Langland Bay. Park above the bay.

Facilities Shops above the beach, more comprehensive facilities, including surf shops, in Mumbles (see Appendix). Lifeguards in summer.

To the east of Crab Island are a couple of breaks that are seldom surfed, as they require a very big swell to work. There's a right-hander breaking off the rocks at BRACELET POINT (GR 629870) into Bracelet Bay towards mid tide, but it needs a big SW swell to start to work. NW winds are offshore here.

2 LANGLAND
➤ *Landranger 159, GR 607874*

Surf Langland is almost always crowded when there's a swell running, when a very high standard of surfing may be found here. There are three breaks: 'Lefts' and 'Middle of Bay' being beach breaks that work right through the tide, giving both lefts and rights. There's also 'Reef', which has lefts and rights from mid tide up. The waves here work in all winds except SE or E.

Access & Facilities See Crab Island.

3 LANGLAND POINT
➤ *Landranger 159, GR 605869*

Surf A right-hand point break on the west side of Langland Bay. It breaks over rocks, and can hold a good-sized wave on a big swell. It only works at low tide, when long rides are possible. When conditions are less than perfect, you may find it has a tendency to close out. Winds from N to NW are offshore. Not a beginner's wave.

Access There's a track out to the point from Langland Bay.

Facilities None at the break - see Crab Island.

4 THE BOILER
➤ *Landranger 159, GR 598868*

Surf A fast, shallow right-hand point break over rocks. Works on a big W swell at low tide. It tends to be somewhat inconsistent, but when it's working at its best The Boiler is an exciting wave. For experienced surfers only! N to NW winds are offshore.

Access The Boiler is at Whiteshell Point, mid way between Langland Bay and Caswell Bay, reached by a track along the coast.

Facilities None - see Langland Bay, Crab Island or Caswell Bay.

5 CASWELL BAY
➤ *Landranger 158, GR 595875*

Surf A popular beach break which can get very crowded. There are both lefts and rights here, often with very good shape. The lefts are best and can get pretty hollow at times. This break only works for a couple of hours either side of high tide, when the bay is actually split into two seperate bays by the rising tide. N to NE winds are offshore. On spring tides it doesn't work too well. Popular with beginners and canoeists.

Access The B4593 runs above the beach. There's a large car park here.

Facilities Shops and refreshments available above the beach. Lifeguards patrol the beach in summer.

6 PWLLDU POINT
➤ *Landranger 159 GR 574864*

Surf A point break with a selection of right-handers breaking over a rocky bottom. The bigger waves break further out around the point. It's a long paddle out from the beach; you may have to contend with a sideshore rip when you get out to the line-up. Not a place for inexperienced surfers. Best from low to mid tide on an incoming tide. Winds from a N'ly quarter are offshore.

Access It's a long walk to this break. There's limited parking above the NE side of Pwlldu Bay,

Left: A heavy winter wave at Aberavon
Below: 'Guts' Griffiths, Langland

but if this is full you may have to park back down the road in Pyle. There's a track down the cliffs to the pleasant secluded bay, walk to the SW end of it and paddle out (paddling out is easier than clambering over the rocks to the point).

Facilities   None, the nearest are in Pyle village.

7 ROACHES / SECRET REEF
➤ *Landranger 159, GR 566864*

Surf   A reef break over rock which may have a wave on small swells. It can get quite hollow, but breaks in shallow water. Works from low to mid tide. Best in calm conditions or in light winds. Experienced surfers only.

Access   From Hunts Bay along coast path.

Facilities   None.

8 HUNTS BAY
➤ *Landranger 159, GR 563867*

Surf   There are two breaks here, a left-hand reef break and a right-hand point. Both break over rock. The left picks up more swell than the right and can produce a hollow wave which wraps into the bay in

very shallow water. It works at low tide only, but when the tide gets too high you can move over to the right, which works from mid to high tide (although as mentioned above, it does need a larger swell to produce a wave). When it's working well, the right can have a well lined-up wall which is very fast, but it may get so fast it becomes nothing more than a close-out.

The bay is very exposed to W and SW winds, which easily spoil the surf, but it is sheltered from the NW. Winds from N to NE are offshore. Getting in and out of the water can be a tricky business, especially on a big swell. This is definitely not a spot for inexperienced surfers.

Access   From the village of Southgate there's a minor road SE leading to Hunts Farm above the bay. Drive out here, park by the side of the road, and walk down the cliff path to the break.

Facilities   None, nearest are in Southgate.

9 POBBLES BEACH
➤ *Landranger 159, GR 541875*

Surf   Pobbles is the beach to the east of Threecliff Bay on the opposite side of the Pennard Pill estuary.

Empty high tide Gower reef

There are two breaks here, a mid tide beach break, and at low tide a short left-hand point break over a reef on the east side of the beach. The left is the better of the two breaks. Not a great break and usually smaller than nearby Threecliff. The beach break is OK for beginners.

Access Either from the car park in Pennard Golf Course above the beach, or from Threecliff Bay.

Facilities None.

10 THREECLIFF BAY
➤ *Landranger 159, GR 535877*

Surf A good quality beach break, often hollow, and not usually too crowded. It's best at high tide, although it does work right through from low tide. N to NNE winds are offshore. It's quite well sheltered from W and NW winds by the Great Tor cliffs above the beach. OK for beginners.

Access From the A4118 at Penmaen a lane leads to a steep path down the cliff to the beach, and there's another path from Parkmill, about a mile east of Penmaen. You can also walk here from Oxwich Bay.

Facilities None other than the scenery. Threecliff Bay is a very picturesque sandy bay ringed by cliffs on which are the ruins of Pennard Castle. It gets it's name from a three-pointed outcrop of rock projecting from the cliffs on the E side of the bay. At low tide, Threecliff links with Oxwich Bay to give a 3 mile long crescent of sand.

Accommodation There's a caravan park and camp site above the western side of the bay, just inside the river mouth.

11 OXWICH BAY
➤ *Landranger 159, GR 510870*

Surf A SE-facing bay that is sheltered when everywhere else is being hammered by a big SW storm swell. It's a popular high tide break, with beach break peaks along the length of the bay giving lefts and rights which can often have good shape and be pretty hollow. It needs a big swell from the W, SW, or S to work, and only works at high tide. Usually at its best as the tide starts to drop. It's often quite crowded.

There are also peaks to be found from mid to high tide further east along the beach below Nicholaston Burrows, around the mouth of the Nicholaston Pill. A good option if you want a less crowded surf, but the waves may not be of such good quality as those at Oxwich or Threecliff.

NW winds are offshore at Oxwich Bay, although W winds are also OK at the western end of the bay. In strong W'ly winds the cliffs above Oxwich Point provide good shelter, but the breaks further east will be more exposed.

This is a good beach for beginners. Bear in mind its popularity and keep out of the way of more experienced surfers.

Access There's a turn-off from the A4118 to Oxwich village, and there's a car park next to the dunes of Oxwich Burrows which are right above the bay. You can walk along from Threecliff Bay at low tide.

Facilities Food kiosk at the car park, and cafes and a shop in the village. The Oxwich Bay Hotel at the eastern end of the beach also does meals and bar snacks. The beach is patrolled by lifeguards in summer. There's a windsurfing school on the beach if you want to try something different.

Accommodation There's a caravan park and camp site above Oxwich Burrows, and a camp site in the village.

12 OXWICH POINT (INSIDE)
➤ *Landranger 159, GR 514850*

Surf A rocky right-hand point break which will work on a smaller swell than Oxwich Point, although it still needs a good sized W'ly swell to work. It won't hold as large a wave as the outside point, but it's a fast wave and can get quite hollow. NW winds are offshore, but the headland gives some protection from W'ly winds. Not a wave for novices.

Access Park in the car park at Oxwich village, from where it's about a mile walk to the break.

Facilities None, nearest are in Oxwich.

13 OXWICH POINT
➤ *Landranger 159, GR 508857*

Surf Like the inside point, this is also a rocky right-hand point break working on a big W'ly swell, but it can hold a much bigger wave. On a really big swell it will occasionally link up with the inside wave to give a fast ride with a number of hollow sections. Best at low tide, when it can produce one of the best waves in the area. NW winds are offshore. A wave for experienced surfers only.

Access & Facilities   See Oxwich Point (inside)

14 SLADE BAY / BOOT REEF
➤ *Landranger 159, GR 487854*

Surf   A beach and reef break in the small bay known as 'The Sands'. I don't have much information on this spot, as it's not often surfed because there are plenty of other waves in the area that are better and more accessible. It needs a big SW or W swell to work. N to NE winds are offshore.

Access   There's a road out to the hamlet of Slade from Oxwich. Park here and take the path down to the beach.

Facilities   None.

15 HORTON BEACH
➤ *Landranger 159, 478855*

Surf   A beach break, rights and lefts, which works on a good SW swell. When the swell gets bigger than six feet, however, it will start to close out. Close-outs can also be a problem if the banks aren't lined-up properly. Best from mid to high tide. Winds from N are offshore. Not really an ideal beginner's wave.

Access   Easily reached from the village of Horton, just above the beach.

Facilities   In Horton.

16 PORT EYNON BAY
➤ *Landranger 159, GR 474852*

Surf   An inferior beach break, at the SW end of the beach, which is only really worth a visit on a big swell when better breaks are out of control. It breaks both left and right, but mainly right. Only works at low tide. NW winds are offshore. OK for beginners.

Access   Easily reached from the village of Port Eynon at the end of the A4118. There's a large car park behind the dunes.

Facilities   Shop, cafe, and toilets above the beach.

Lifeguards patrol the beach. Port Eynon is at the southern end of the South Gower Coast Nature Reserve, which stretches for six miles NW to Worms Head.

Accommodation   There are a number of caravan parks and camp sites in and around Port Eynon. There is also a youth hostel.

17 PORT EYNON POINT
➤ *Landranger 159, GR 465844*

Surf   A right hand reef break for competent surfers only. It comprises a steep, sucky take off, and a short, fast, and often hollow ride. It can work up to well overhead. Best at low tide. It's OK in light N winds.

Access   Take the path to the headland from the car park at the S end of Port Eynon.

Facilities   See Port Eynon Bay.

18 SUMPTERS
➤ *Landranger 159, GR 463846*

Surf   A good right hand reef break, with poorer lefts, which will hold just about any size swell from three feet up. Best from low to mid tide, in calm conditions. It's also OK in N to NE winds which are offshore. Sheltered from NW winds. Not a wave for inexperienced surfers.

Access   You can reach the break from the end of various roads around the Port Eynon/Overton area and it's not far from Port Eynon Point. The break itself is reached by walking out along the sewer pipe in the gulley in front of the break. From there it's an easy paddle out.

Facilities   None, the nearest are in Port Eynon/Overton.

19 BOILER LEFT
➤ *Landranger 159, GR 444853*

Surf   As the name implies, a left hand reef break,

Oxwich Bay

which can be of excellent quality and very hollow. There's also a shorter right too. Breaks on most swells, but will close-out once it gets over about eight feet. Works from low through to about mid tide. Like many of the south Gower reefs it's at its best in calm conditions, but it's also OK in light NE and NW winds. For experienced surfers only.

Access   Drive to the end of the road at Overton, then take the cliff top path as far as the valley below 'Common Cliff' (on OS map). The break is at the end of this valley.

Facilities   None.

20 PETE'S REEF
➤ *Landranger 159, GR 437857*

Surf `A very popular left and right-hand reef break, which picks up just about any swell going. Both the left and right are fast and hollow, but short. Works at low tide. Best when conditions are glassy, or with light winds from N. Another break for experienced surfers only.

Access   Half a mile NW of Boiler Left.

Facilities   None.

21 MEWSLADE REEF
➤ *Landranger 159, GR 415873*

Surf   A left and right-hand reef break working on a good-sized swell from W, SW, or S. The lefts are better and often hollow. Works at low tide. Winds from N are offshore, but W winds are funnelled down the valley above the break and are almost offshore. Once again, a wave for experienced surfers only. Less experienced surfers may find a wave breaking in Mewslade Bay at low tide which is more suitable for learning on.

Access   There' a turn-off from the B4247 just before Rhossili at Middleton. Park at the end of the road, then follow the path through the fields to Mewslade Bay. The break is at the west end of the bay. There are also paths to Mewslade Bay from Pitton and Rhossili.

Facilities   None.

22 FALL BAY
➤ *Landranger 159, GR413873*

Surf   On a good swell, short punchy beach break waves, lefts and rights, can be found in Fall Bay, which is essentially a western extension of Mewslade Bay. It works from mid to high tide, so is an alternative once the tide gets too high for Mewslade Reef. The waves, however, are of not such good quality. N to NW winds are offshore. The cliffs give protection from W winds.

Access   See Mewslade Reef.

Facilities   None.

23 CRABART
➤ *Landranger 159, GR402868*

Surf   A fickle, shallow, right-hand reef break. Can be fast and hollow when it's working well, but backwash from the cliffs can easily spoil it. Only surfable at low tide. Winds from N are offshore. Definitely not a wave for novices.

Access   Take the road from Rhossili out towards Worms Head and park. From here there's a 15-minute walk out to the headland to check the break - bad news if it's not working!

Facilities   None, the nearest are in Rhossili.

24 RHOSSILI
➤ *Landranger 159, GR 410895*

Surf   The southern extension of the huge sweep of beach that stretches north towards Llangennith. The S end of the beach picks up less swell than the N, but the left and right-hand beach breaks to be found here are good for beginners. It's also an option for more experienced surfers if the surf is closing out at Llangennith. The very south end of the beach is sheltered from strong S and SE winds by the cliffs. E to SE winds are offshore.

Access   Straightforward access from Rhossili, where there's car parking.

Facilities   Shops, cafes and pubs in Rhossili.

25 LLANGENNITH (HILLEND)
➤ *Landranger 159, GR 410910*

Surf One of the most popular spots on the Gower which suits beginners and experts alike. A consistent beach break with left and right-hand peaks all the way along the beach, it works on swells from any direction, and is always crowded when there's a good swell running, especially in summer. Works at all stages of the tide. N, NE, and SE winds are offshore, but it can also hold a surfable wave in onshore conditions. Once the waves get over 5ft the paddle out, through line after line of white water, can be very hard work.

Access Reached from Llangennith (follow signs to the beach). The road to the beach is very narrow and twisty. Parking (charge in summer) is through the caravan park and camp site in the dunes. From here it's a short walk to the beach.

Facilities Shops, pubs, surf hire and surf shop (see Appendix) in Llangennith, also a shop at the top of the car park. There'a a BSA surf school at Hillend Caravan Park offering both group and individual tuition in the summer.

Accommodation Hillend Caravan Park above the beach has a good range of facilities and is probably one of the best bases for anyone visiting Gower.

26 PEAKS, THREE PEAKS, BURRY HOLMS
➤ *Landranger 159, GR 400925*

Surf Probably the most consistent beach break in the area. Peaks picks up any swell and is usually bigger and better than the breaks to the south at Llangennith. There are three distinct peaks, all left and right, but the rights tend to be better, and are often long, fast, and hollow when conditions are right. They break right through the tide (except on spring high tides). Offshore winds are from NE through to SE. The high quality of the waves ensures that the water is usually crowded.

Access A 15-minute walk north from Hillend, see Llangennith.

Facilities None, see Llangennith.

27 SHEEP'S JAW
➤ *Landranger 159, GR 404927*

Surf An unremarkable left and right-hand break just around the north corner of Rhossili Bay. Its only redeeming feature is that it's sheltered from SW winds, otherwise all the other local breaks are better. Works at low tide. S to SE winds are offshore.

Access See Peaks. At low tide you can walk through the gap between Burry Holms and the 'mainland' to the break.

Facilities None, see Llangennith.

28 BROUGHTON POINT
➤ *Landranger 159, GR 413933*

Surf This is a left-hand, sand bottom, point break at the SW end of Broughton Bay at the spot marked 'Foxhole Point' on the OS map. It works on a big W swell, when it can give long rides. It works for around an hour either side of high tide, but not on small tides. S to SE winds are offshore. There's a slight rip taking you away from the line-up. Beginners are advised to stick to the beach at Llangennith rather than surf here.

Access Easily reached from the caravan park at Burry Holms, which is about one mile north of Llangennith village.

Facilities Refreshments available at caravan park or in Llangennith.

Accommodation Caravan park above the beach.

10 PEMBROKESHIRE

Pembrokeshire has a distinct N-S divide, with the south generally having more consistent and larger surf than the north coast which is not so exposed to swells. Freshwater West, in south Pembrokeshire, is probably the most consistent beach in Wales.

Pembrokeshire picks up much the same swell as Cornwall, Devon, and the rest of the south Wales coast, but the strong tides in the Bristol Channel, particularly those around St David's Head, affect it and ensure that the surf is always about a couple of

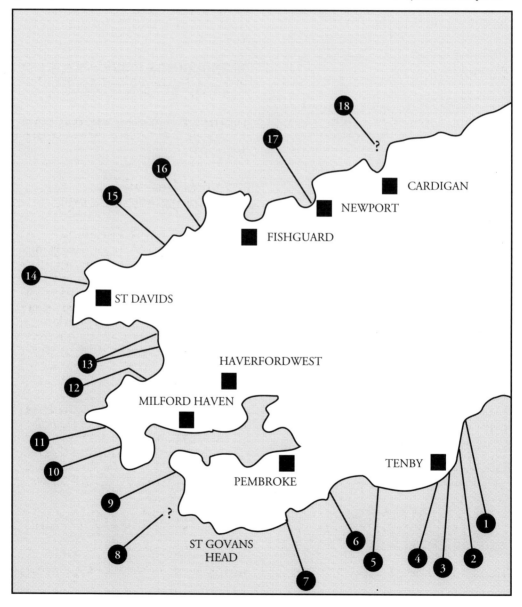

18

17

16

15

CARDIGAN

NEWPORT

14

FISHGUARD

ST DAVIDS

13

HAVERFORDWEST

12

MILFORD HAVEN

11

10

TENBY

9

PEMBROKE

1

8

ST GOVANS
HEAD

6

5

4

3

2

7

feet smaller than that to be found in Cornwall or Devon.

There's a possibility of surf when low pressure systems have taken up station anywhere in the Atlantic, but you won't get waves with much size unless the low is deeper than 990mb. The further north the depression the deeper it will need to be to produce waves.

Winds from the SW and W, the prevailing direction, are onshore at most breaks; winds from S to N you'll find give offshore conditions at many breaks. NW winds are usually bad news as they tend to blow the surf flat or spoil it at most breaks, although there are exceptions.

CLIMATE

Water temperatures are similar to those of the rest of SW Britain, with the Gulf Stream having a major warming effect. Average temperatures in winter vary from 7-9°C (46-48°F); in summer they rise to an average of l6-l7°C (60-63°F). Winter air temperatures are generally quite mild, around 9-10°C (46-48°F), whilst summer temperatures average around 21°C (70°F). A 5/3mm steamer, gloves, boots and maybe a hood will be needed for winter. A 3mm steamer will do for the summer or a spring suit on the warmest days.

There are no real hazards in the water apart from weever fish, which lurk on the sea floor off sandy beaches in shallow water. They can give a bad sting which may need professional attention. It's very common to find seals out in the line-up, and you may see dolphins, porpoises, and basking sharks.

As with SW England and South Wales, there are very big tidal ranges in Pembrokeshire - some springs exceed seven metres - and these naturally affect the surf. If a break is recommended as being best at a particular stage of the tide, get there then; there may be nothing at all at other stages!

Sea pollution is seldom a major problem in Pembrokeshire. There may be oil spills from the oil terminals in Milford Haven estuary, but these rarely affect the coastline - not that that makes them any more acceptable.

Most of the Pembrokeshire coastline is within the Pembrokeshire Coast National Park and receives special protection as a designated Heritage Coast.

The breaks are described from E to W.

1 WISEMAN'S BRIDGE
➤ *Landranger 158, GR 146060*

Surf A right-hander breaking over sand and rock, best around high tide. It only works on a big swell and winds from W-NW are offshore. Predominantly a winter break. The coastline to the E of Wiseman's Bridge is also worth checking for surf on a big swell combined with winds from NW-NE. There are breaks to be found near Amroth, for instance.

Access Wiseman's Bridge is on the Amroth - Saundersfoot coastal road. There is space to park above the beach.

Facilities Plenty of shops, pubs and cafes in nearby Saundersfoot. The Sands nightclub is a popular spot for a bit of late night action, especially in summer.

Accommodation There are plenty of caravan parks and camp sites in the area, plus a youth hostel just outside the town.

2 MONKSTONE POINT
➤ *Landranger 158, GR 150032*

Surf This is a point break at the S end of Saundersfoot beach, which can give an excellent, long right-hander, breaking over a sand and boulder bottom on a good swell. However, it does require a very big swell to work. It's one of the few breaks in Pembrokeshire that are offshore in a W to SW wind, and on a big S or SW swell. When everywhere else is blown out it may be worth a visit. It may require constant paddling to stay in the line-up, so, for this reason, it's not really suitable for beginners unless the waves are pretty small.

Access This starts at the turn-off to a caravan site just before the roundabout at New Hedges on the junction of the B4316 with the A487. Park near the farm above the site and walk down to the headland, then down the cliffs to the break. Alternatively you can make the long walk along the beach from either Saundersfoot or Tenby.

Facilities None near the break - see Wiseman's Bridge or Tenby.

Accommodation See Wiseman's Bridge or Tenby.

Freshwater East

3 TENBY NORTH BEACH
➤ Landranger 158, GR 134010

Surf Not often surfed as it requires a very big swell
to throw up any sort of quality wave. There's a right
that breaks off the lifeboat slipway - once again, a
very big swell is needed. W to NW winds are
offshore. No good at high tide due to backwash.

Access The A478 takes you into Tenby. The
narrow streets make it a frustrating place to drive
through, especially when it's heaving with tourists.
There's a one-way system through the town. Park as
near the beach as you can - you'll have to pay.

Facilities Everything you'd expect in the county's
major tourist resort. Fortunately, despite the
commercialism, Tenby has retained much of its
charm, and it's probably one of the most picturesque
harbours in Wales. The nightlife here is pretty good
in summer. There are two surf shops in Tenby (see
Appendix).

Accommodation Plenty of everything - caravan
parks and camp sites, hotels, and a youth hostel just
inland of Saundersfoot.

4 TENBY, SOUTH BEACH
➤ Landranger 158, GR 130000

Surf A better bet than the North Beach. On a big
swell you can sometimes find a good beach break
here. At its best it can produce steep, fast waves,
both left and right, and sometimes quite hollow. It's
best just after high tide, although it will work from
mid tide up. Winds from W through to N are
offshore. OK for beginners.

Access, Facilities and Accommodation Good-sized
car park above the beach. Also see Tenby North
Beach.

5 MANORBIER
➤ Landranger 158, GR 060975

Surf A small, scenic bay, which has a good right
breaking off the cliff at the W end of the bay. The

right breaks over a rock reef, then on to a sand bottom. Best just after high tide, although it can work right through the tide. A NE wind is preferable, but it also works in N and NW winds. There are also waves in the middle and on the left of the bay as the tide recedes.

It can be crowded here and it's becoming increasingly popular with surfers from as far away as the Gower and South Wales. The beach breaks are OK for beginners.

Access The B4585 runs into Manorbier from the A4139. There are signs in the village to the beach. Car park in the valley behind the beach.

Facilities None at the beach - shops and pubs in village.

Accommodation Camp sites are to be found in abundance around Tenby. There is a youth hostel at nearby Shrinkle Haven.

6 FRESHWATER EAST
➤ Landranger 158, GR 020980

Surf A very attractive sweep of beach, facing SE. It requires a big swell before it starts to work, but when it does it can provide some nice fast beach breaks, which can be quite long and hollow. Works best from high to mid tide. It's another beach worth visiting if SW winds are blowing out a big swell elsewhere. If Broadhaven South is too big it will be smaller here. NW to W winds are offshore. OK for beginners.

Access The 4584 runs into the village from the A4139. There are signs to the beach. Car parking in the dunes.

Facilities A beach shop in the dunes above the beach, otherwise you'll have to go into the village.

Acommodation Camp sites locally.

7 BROADHAVEN SOUTH
➤ Landranger 158, GR 980940

Surf A high tide beach break with punchy, hollow peaks wedging up off the cliff wall and sandbanks. Gives a short but fast ride, when it's often possible to get tubed. It needs a good sized S or SW swell to work. When it does, it has the advantage of being one of the few breaks in the county that's offshore in W to NW winds. For this reason it can often be crowded when the breaks to the W and N are blown out. Not really a beginner's wave.

Access From the B4319 Castlemartin road there's a signposted turn-off to the village of Bosherston. A lane leads you to a National Trust car park above the beach.

Facilities Toilets at the car park. Nearest facilities are in the village (limited).

Accommodation Limited local accommodation, but plenty around Tenby.

8 SPOT X

Surf Somewhere in this area is a wave that has been described as one of the best reef breaks in Britain on it's day. However, I know that no one in Pembrokeshire will thank me for mentioning it and as access is extremely restricted, this is one wave that I'm afraid you'll have to discover for yourself.

9 FRESHWATER WEST
➤ Landranger 158, GR 885000

Surf There can't be a surfer in Pembrokeshire who hasn't surfed at 'Fresh' at one time or another, as this is the spot everyone heads for if the surf at their home break is too small. It's also the regular venue for the Welsh Amateur Surfing Championships. If it's flat here then it's unlikely you'll find a wave anywhere in the county. The good thing about Freshwater is that it's a big beach with peaks all along its length, so if you're prepared to walk a few hundred yards you can usually avoid the crowds.

The authorities seem to have made every attempt to put you off surfing here. Red flags seem to be flying constantly; there are signs warning that bathing here is 'dangerous and irresponsible' due to the currents and quicksands and there even used to be a sign with the exotic legend 'Beware of snakes'! (this refers to adders, which are common in Pembrokeshire). Add to this the detonations from the Castlemartin firing range behind the beach, and you might be justified in thinking you were dicing with death just by paying a visit to the beach.

However, it's a pleasant enough spot to spend a day in summer - especially if there's a good swell running - and it can produce some good quality, powerful, and often quite large waves. There will be left and right-hand peaks all along the beach depending on the condition of the banks, with waves at most stages of the tide.

To the S end of the beach there's a good peak in front of the rocks at 'Little Furzenip' at low tide, and just S of here in what's known as Middle Bay there's a good right and a left over rocks and sand at high tide. Winds from E to NE are offshore. It can also be OK in SE'lys.

A longshore S rip can be a problem at Fresh, especially on bigger swells, and inexperienced surfers should be aware of this. They would also be advised to steer clear of the breaks close to or over rocks at the S end of the beach.

Access   The B4320 from Pembroke takes you to the N end of the beach, and the B4319 from Pembroke to the S end. Parking above the beach at either end.

Facilities   Toilet block in main car park above beach, and sometimes an ice cream van in summer. Otherwise nearest refreshments are in the pub at Castlemartin. There's a surf shop in Pembroke (see Appendix).

Accommodation   Not a great deal until you get to Pembroke or Tenby.

Autumn swell, Freshwater West

10 WEST DALE
➤ *Landranger 157 GR 798058*

Surf   A powerful beach break that picks up quite a lot of swell. There's a good right off the cliffs at low tide and a left on the other side of the beach as the tide rises. It works best from low to mid tide. The constant shifting of the sand banks can affect the quality of the waves. There are rock outcrops dotted about on the beach which you must avoid. NE winds are offshore, but the high cliffs on either side of the bay provide some protection from cross-shore winds too. Not an ideal beach for beginners.

Access   The B4327 from Haverfordwest runs through Dale, from where you follow the one way system up towards the castle and out to the bay. The road here is very narrow, and there's very limited parking space above the beach, which is reached by a footpath through fields from the road.

Facilities   None, the nearest are in Dale, including West Wales Windsurfing School, who also stock a certain amount of surfing equipment.

Accommodation   Caravan park at Marloes. More caravan parks and camp sites along the coast towards Broadhaven. Youth hostels at Marloes and Broadhaven.

11 MARLOES
➤ *Landranger 157 GR 780070*

Surf   Marloes beach is arguably the most impressive in Pembrokeshire, and due to it's relative isolation, size and awkward access, it's unlikely crowds will ever be a problem here.
The beach faces SW and picks up swells from SW-W, with breaks all along the beach at most stages of the tide. Winds from N-E are offshore. Not recommended for beginners due to it's isolation. Watch you don't get cut off at high tide.

Access   Follow signs from Marloe village. Large National Trust carpark above the beach, it's a 10 minute walk form the carpark.

Facilities   None

Accomodation   Youth hostel above the beach.

12 BROADHAVEN
➤ *Landranger 157 GR 860136*

Surf   Broad Haven can produce some reasonably good left and right-hand beach breaks on a good swell, and they can be pretty hollow too. It tends to be better on a rising tide and best of all at high tide. It may well repay a visit when beaches such as Newgale and Whitesands are too big or closing out. E-SE winds are offshore. OK for beginners.

Access   The B4341 from Haverfordwest runs into the village.There's also a very narrow, twisting coastal road, with some very steep gradients, from Newgale. Car parking above the beach.

Facilities   Pubs serving bar meals above the beach, also shops, although they may not all be open in winter. There's a surf shop above the beach (see Appendix).

Acommodation   There are caravan parks and camp sites at Broad Haven, Little Haven, and Hasguard Cross (also see Newgale). There's a youth hostel in Broad Haven.

13 NEWGALE
➤ *Landranger 157 GR 850210*

Surf   A magnificent stretch of beach, with peaks all along and easy access. The size of the beach means

Lines as far as the eye can see, dawn, St Bride's Bay

crowds are rarely a problem. The waves vary depending on the state of the sandbanks; they often have a tendency to back off unless the swell has a bit of poke to it. When it gets overhead it can be difficult to get out through the numerous lines of white water. However, on a nice clean 4 to 5ft swell, Newgale can be great fun and can sometimes put up waves with good long walls on them. It's not usually too good on low tide, and backwash off the pebble bank at the top of the beach spoils the waves at high tide, but there are waves at all stages in between. E to NE winds are offshore. A popular beach with beginners, windsurfers, swimmers and canoeists.

Access   The A487 Haverfordwest-St David's road runs alongside the beach, with plenty of parking above it.

Facilities   There's a surf shop based at the garage in front of the beach, which also hires out equipment. There's also a supermarket, cafe and the Duke of Edinburgh pub adjacent to the garage. Toilets are above the beach at the N end and there's a cafe and toilets at the S end.

Accommodation   There's a large caravan park and camp site right in front of the beach at the N end, well situated for pub and shop: popular with visiting surfers. There's another caravan park at the S end. Youth hostels are at Broad Haven, Pen-y-Cwm and St David's.

14 WHITESANDS
➤ *Landranger 157 GR 732270*

Surf   When it's working Whitesands is a very pleasant beach to surf, surrounded by impressive scenery; however the surf is rather over rated. There are peaks all along the beach, which shift around depending on the banks, but usually tend to be better at the N end. It's generally better just after high tide to around mid tide. A couple of hours before low tide, there's sometimes a right hander (The Elevator) breaking off the small headland at the N end of the beach. There's also a rip here, which on a big swell provides an easy means of getting out (although there are a few rocks to negotiate on the paddle out). Beginners should keep well away from this. It's best in winds from NE to SE, with E being directly offshore.

Whitesands is always smaller than Freshwater West, and often Newgale too, because the swell is blocked by Ramsey Island and deflected by the strong tidal flows around St David's Head.

The author gets some mini-mal action, Whitesands

This is a very popular beach with beginners and just about every form of surf-riding vehicle known to man can be found here on a busy day in summer. The problem has become so bad recently that an advisory leaflet aimed at canoeists and other inexperienced 'surfers' (I use the term loosely) is now available free from the lifeguards. Please get one if you fall into these categories!

Access   The B4583 turn-off from the A487, just outside St David's, leads to the large car park above the beach. Queues and lack of spaces can be a problem in summer.

Facilities   There's a well-stocked beach shop, surf hire, and lifeguards at the beach in summer. Also a toilet block at the top of the car park. Ma Sime's Surf Hut in St Davids can supply just about anything you need for surf trip.
   There's a lot to do around St David's if it's flat. You can wander around the Cathedral and Bishop's Palace, visit one of the aquariums, hire a mountain bike and see some of the countryside, or take a walk around the coast or up Carn Llidi, the hill above the beach from which there are tremendous views.

Accommodation   There are caravan parks and camp sites above the beach, and plenty more around St David's. There's a youth hostel about a mile from the beach.

15 ABEREIDDY
➤ *Landranger 157 GR 797314*

Surf   A small black-sand bay, with a left breaking over rocks at the S end of the bay, which on a big swell can be very fast and heavy. There's also a generally inferior right on the opposite side of the bay and occasional peaks in the middle. Can work at most stages of the tide, but it varies depending on conditions. E to NE winds are offshore. The beach breaks are OK for beginners. The left should be surfed by experienced surfers only.

Access   There's a signposted turn-off from the A487 St David's-Fishguard road at Croesgoch. Park above the beach.

Facilities   There may be an ice cream van in the car park in summer. The nearest shops and pub are in Croesgoch. The Sloop Inn at the picturesque harbour of Porthgain is also quite close.

Accommodation   Caravan parks and camp sites locally. Youth hostel at Trevine.

It can get even better than this - but not often. **Abereiddy, winter swell**

16 ABERMAWR
➤ *Landranger 157 GR 882346*

Surf This is a very fickle beach, and will only work well on a very big swell. There's a right off the cliffs at the NE end of the bay, sometimes a peak in the middle, and a left at the SW end. The SW end is sheltered by cliffs from strong S and SE winds. All the breaks work a couple of hours before and after low tide and are very much dependant upon the height of the tide as to whether there's a wave or not. At neaps the water may not fall far enough for the breaks to work properly.

As the tide comes in, it can be tricky getting out of the water, because the waves dump on the steep pebble bank and there's a strong backwash. Beginners should be careful when surfing here.

If you arrive here and see good waves from the cliff top, go down to the beach and double-check before struggling into your wetsuit - it's always smaller than it looks from the cliff.

Access There's a signposted turn-off to Abermawr about one mile NE of Mathry. Limited roadside parking above the beach.

Facilities None

Accommodation A number of caravan parks and camp sites within easy reach. Youth hostel on the coast just N of St Nicholas and at Trevine.

Spot Z

17 NEWPORT
➤ *Landranger 145 GR 050400*

Surf Newport is very rarely surfed, mainly because it needs a huge swell to work, and when it does work there are other beaches nearer to the surfing centres of Pembrokeshire that will probably be better. It's a long, sweeping beach facing NW, with beach breaks along the length of it. There can be waves at most stages of the tide. E to SE winds are offshore.

Access There's a turn-off from the A487 in the centre of Newport down to the beach. Parking above the beach. It's often crowded in summer, as this is a very popular spot with holidaymakers, but it's highly unlikely that you'd get a wave at that time of year.

Facilities Refreshments available above the beach, and in Newport. Toilets above beach. Lifeguards in summer. If it's flat the nearby Preseli Hills are worth a visit.

Accommodation There are two caravan parks and camp sites in Newport.

18 SPOT Z

Surf An excellent right hander that's not quite within Pembrokeshire. However, no one would thank me for giving the name away, so this is one you'll have to find for yourself.

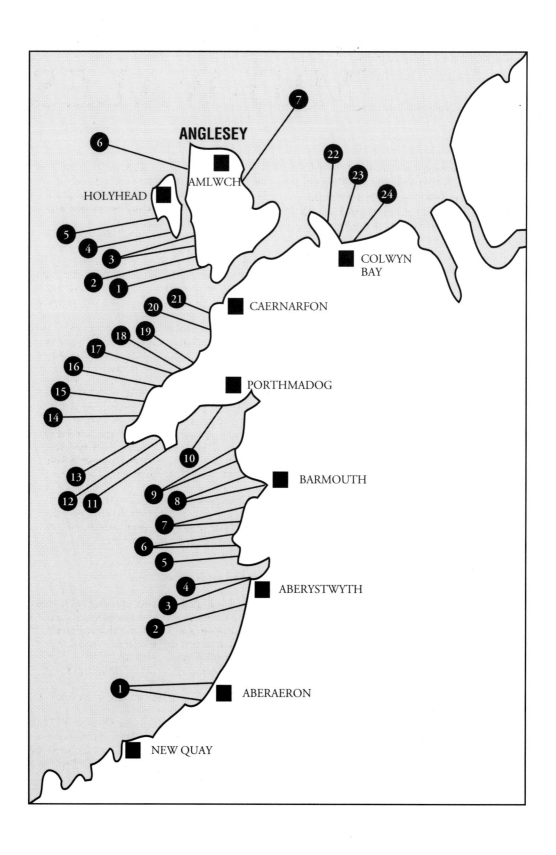

11 NORTH & MID-WALES

North Wales has more consistent surf than Mid-Wales, with Hell's Mouth on the Lleyn Peninsula in particular having been a regular venue for surfers from North Wales and northern England since the 1960s. Other spots in North Wales and Anglesey can also get waves fairly regularly, although nowhere near as often as the breaks in the south of Wales.

Mid-Wales doesn't often get good quality waves, but one thing you can be sure of if you decide to surf here is that you'll almost always be surfing on beaches with impressive backdrops - the Cambrian Mountains rise up inland in Mid-Wales and the mountains of Snowdonia look down on the north coast to give an equally spectacular coastline.

The whole area is generally unspoilt, although there are parts of the north coast such as Llandudno and Colwyn Bay that have been heavily developed for the summer holiday trade. Gwynedd and Anglesey are the most 'Welsh' parts of Wales and you'll frequently hear Welsh being spoken in this area and often in the surf.

With it's superb and varied scenery Mid and North Wales can provide plenty of alternatives if there's no surf when you visit. Climbing or walking are an obvious choice because of the excellent coastline and mountains the area has to offer. Mountain biking is another excellent option.

CLIMATE

The prevailing SW to W airstreams produce a mild, but wet climate. The rain is particularly noticeable over the mountains, where it will often fall as snow in winter.

The water temperature is at its warmest in late summer/early autumn, when it should be about 15 °C (59°F). By late winter/early spring it will be at its coldest, 6°C (43°F). A 5mm steamer, boots, gloves and hat will be necessary in winter, while a 3mm steamer will be adequate from July - September.

The surf will be at its best when there's a deep depression to the south west of Ireland or west of the Bay of Biscay combined with a high pressure system over the UK which gives easterly, offshore winds in the Irish Sea. Any low to the west of the Bay of Biscay that drops below about 990mb may produce a groundswell which hits the area two to three days later.

A low passing over the British Isles will usually see south-westerly gales switch to north-westerly, giving good waves on south-facing beaches. However, if the wind only goes round as far as west it will ruin the waves on just about every beach in the area. The Lleyn Peninsula is best situated to pick up waves under these conditions.

The frequent SW gales that batter Wales at various times throughout the year will also produce surf all along the coast, and this is one of the main sources of waves for Mid Wales surfers.

As with the rest of Britain, autumn, winter, and spring produce the most consistent surf, with autumn being the best time to visit as the air and water temperatures are still quite acceptable. Summer is a great time to see the area, but don't expect much in the way of surf at this time. Flat spells can be long and frequent, especially in Mid Wales, where they may last for several weeks at a time.

Although most of the surfable beaches are generally pretty clean, there can be some pollution throughout the area from agricultural run-off into streams which discharge into the sea.

1 ABERAERON AREA

Surf This area has a number of pebble and boulder points and reefs projecting out to sea which have enormous potential. The catch is that they don't often work because they require an extremely big swell to produce any waves at all.

The following spots can all produce waves, and can all be seen from the road:

ABERAERON - a long left hand point break just to the north of the town.

ABERARTH, LLANON, and LLANRHYSTUD - left and right hand peaks. There are also waves to be found in between these towns. All these breaks are better from low tide up, but don't work at high tide. SE winds are offshore.

Also worth checking to the south are New Quay,

One of the fickle waves of the Aberaeron area

Llangranog, Tresait and Aberporth. They get some shelter from prevailing SW winds, and have a small local surf population.

Access   Pretty straightforward at each spot, although it may involve crossing a field or two.

Facilities & Accommodation   There are shops and pubs in each of the towns mentioned, and caravan parks and camp sites at Aberaeron, Llanon, and Llanrhstud.

2 MORFA BYCHAN
➤ *Landranger 135, GR 563772*

Surf   A rocky beach with a left and right-hand peak at the S end, and a right-hander at the N end. Best from low to mid tide. SE winds are offshore. Be careful when getting in and out of the water as the rocks can be slippery. On occasion it can be bigger than the more popular Harbour Trap just up the coast at Aberystwyth.

Access   Turn off the A487 along a signposted road to the south of Aberystwyth. Park at the caravan site above the beach.

Facilities   There's a shop, cafe, and bar at the caravan site, but they're open only during the summer.

Accommodation   The caravan site is an obvious choice, otherwise try Aberystwyth.

3 ABERYSTWYTH HARBOUR TRAP
➤ *Landranger 135, GR 579810*

Surf   The best and most popular break in the area. There's a small local surf population which fluctuates depending on the number of surfers studying at the university. On a good swell there may be a number of people out here.
     The Trap is a left and right-hand peak breaking over a boulder reef immediately N of the harbour mouth. It's best from low tide to an hour and a half before high. SE to E winds are offshore.
     There's a rip on the south side of the reef which you can use to paddle out: on big days paddle out

from the harbour mouth. Although the rip can prove useful, you should watch out for this and backwash off the harbour wall. Pollution is a problem here as there's a sewage outlet by the harbour mouth.

The Trap isn't a good wave for beginners to learn on.

Access There's parking on the promenade just north of the harbour.

Facilities Aberystwyth is a popular holiday resort and has a wide selection of shops, cafes and pubs within easy reach of the beach. It's far and away the liveliest town for many miles around, so if you're after some nightlife this is your best bet.

Accommodation Camp sites in the surrounding countryside. B & B in the town.

4 ABERYSTWYTH BEACH

Surf There are three breaks here. At the north end of the beach are two seperate peaks with both lefts and rights; one over Queen's Rocks, and another just to the north of this in front of the Seabank Hotel. Both work at low tide; the one over the rocks has a tendency to close out. All three hold a big SW swell. Further down towards the pier, waves may be found breaking on a very big swell. SE to E winds are offshore.

Access Parking available on Marine Terrace above the beach, although it may be crowded in summer.

Facilities & Accommodation See the Harbour Trap.

5 BORTH
➤ Landranger 135, GR 608890

Surf Two breaks here - a left-hand point break off the headland at Upper Borth and peaks further north along the beach which are mainly right handers. The left has the advantage of being sheltered by the headland from SW winds, which are more often than not responsible for the surf to be found here. There's a cross-current from south to north along the beach. E'ly winds are offshore. OK for beginners.

Access There are three turn-offs to Borth from the A487, from south to north these are the B4572, just north of Aberystwyth, and the B4353 at Bow Street and also at Tre'r-ddol. There's a car park above the beach.

Facilities Shops, cafes, and pubs close by. Ynyslas, at the north end of the beach, is a National Nature Reserve.

Accommodation Youth hostel and B & B in the town. Caravan park and camp site to the south at Llandre.

6 ABERDYFI TO TYWYN

As you drive into the picturesque village of ABERDYFI, you'll see the bar at the mouth of the river Dovey, about a mile out to sea. This can hold a big swell, often with offshore winds blowing down the estuary. However, the only way out to the break is by boat. There are strong tidal currents to contend with once you're out there.

Driving north up the coast towards Tywyn good clean waves may be found beyond the sand dunes in front of Aberdyfi golf course. If you want to try your luck here there are a number of good access points and parking facilities.

TYWYN can have good surf, whether it's the angle of the beach (SW facing), or the nearby Sarn Bach Causeway (a rock bank stretching out to sea) pushing the swell in, it's always a couple of feet bigger and more powerful here than anywhere else along the coast until you reach Hell's Mouth on the Lleyn Peninsula.

You can pick your spot along the beach, where the peaks are continuously shifting. One of the most favoured spots is off the slipway at the south end of the promenade.

The best time to surf Tywyn is an hour either side of high tide, with it usually being better on the ebb. On big tides you might have to wait a bit longer as the swells flatten out at high tide under the influence of the backwash from the sea wall. Watch out for groynes.

Average wave size on a good day is 5 to 6ft. On bigger days the beach works right down to low tide, with fast and snappy waves working over the numerous little sand bars that develop over the winter months.

There's good access here, with plenty of parking, public toilets, and a fish and chip shop in summer. If you're intending to stay, the Neptune Hall caravan park overlooks the beach; it has a good clubhouse and facilities.

7 TONFANAU (NORTH TYWYN) TO FAIRBOURNE

This short stretch of coastline is one of the most interesting in the area, with a variety of reef and point breaks when the conditions are right. It tends to be better in winter when strong winds may spoil the swell at Tywyn.

Just north of the Sarn-y-Bwch Causeway (another rocky bank stretching out into Cardigan Bay) the swell is often smoothed off by the protection of the cliffs and the causeway itself to produce good clean waves when everywhere else is blown out.

There are many spots to discover, but the main ones are Dings, Broken Toe, the reef at Allens Sun Beach (a caravan park), and Lefts at LLWYNGWRIL - ask the locals for directions.

Lefts is a perfect point break on a big swell. SW winds are offshore here. On a spring high tide waves will peel down the point for 100 to 200 yards. Although not very fast after the take-off, the walls are usually long and straight. There are several boulders which provide something of a hazard. A wave for experienced surfers only. There are very few facilities in the area apart from the caravan parks in summer, and the local village store.

Just up the coast, Fairbourne is a really sheltered spot, ideally suited to beginners. There's good access to the beach and a car park.

8 BARMOUTH TO SHELL ISLAND

There are waves on the sand bar about a mile out from the mouth of the river Mawddach at Barmouth, and they're often double the size of anything breaking on the beaches in the area. The currents out here are very strong and you really need a boat to get out to the waves. The strong current makes it very difficult to stay in the line-up.

9 SHELL ISLAND TO HARLECH

Under the right conditions Llandanwg can be a good wave in winter, holding quite clean waves up to about 8ft in rough conditions. There's good access to the beach here from the A496 Barmouth-Harlech road, with a car park just behind the beach. There's a right-hander breaking into the river mouth an hour either side of high tide.

Harlech beach can look good from the road, but you'll find that the waves are usually lacking in power and not very steep. It may be worth checking out when the waves are too big everywhere else.

There are a number of caravan parks and camp sites in the area, and a youth hostel just inland at Llanbedr.

10 CRICCIETH
➤ *Landranger 124, GR 510380*

Surf This is a south-facing beach break, which picks up S and SW swells, although when it's working here it will usually be better elsewhere out on the Lleyn Peninsula. There are beach breaks at all stages of the tide and a heavy peak near the harbour wall on a big swell. Winds from N-NE are offshore. OK for beginners.

Access The A497 from Porthmadoc runs past the beach. From the north the B4911 runs into Criccieth.

Facilities Plenty of shops, cafe and pubs in the town. Surf shop.

Accommodation Numerous caravan parks and camp sites and there's a Butlin holiday camp at Pwllheli.

11 PORTH CEIRIAD
➤ *Landranger 123, GR 310250*

Surf One of the best beach breaks on the Lleyn Peninsula, situated in a secluded cove. It can provide a fast, hollow wave on small to moderate sized swells. Best at high tide. NW to N winds are offshore. OK for beginners.

Access Follow signs for 'Nant-y-big camping'. The roads are single track and twisty, so watch out for oncoming vehicles and farm animals.

Facilities None.

Accommodation Camping above the beach at Nant-y-big.

12 PORTH NEIGWL / HELL'S MOUTH
➤ *Landranger 123, GR 285265*

Surf The best-known surf spot in North Wales, picking up most swells from a S or SW'ly direction.

Hell's Mouth is an impressive four-mile long bay with peaks along its length on a good swell. In small conditions, however, the best chance of a wave will be in the SE corner of the bay under the cliffs, where a good left breaks at low tide: it can have long walls.

Two hundred yards further along the shore there's a good right-hander breaking over a rock outcrop at high tide.

As you move further NW along the bay the waves become smaller although, on a small swell, there may be waves in the centre of the bay in front of the car park.

If the surf in the corner is too big, it may be worth heading towards the NW end of the bay (Rhiw) in search of smaller waves. This is best at high tide. The corner is best in E winds, although it will also hold its shape in light onshore winds. The NW end of the bay is best in NW winds. OK for beginners, although there's a rip to watch out for along the cliffs by the corner. Beginners tend to surf 'in the middle' at Hell's Mouth.

Access   There's access to the NW end of the beach from the Abersoch to Aberdaron road, but most people make for the opposite end which is reached along the road from Llanengan, a hamlet to the SW of Abersoch. There's a car park above the beach at this end.

Facilities   None at the beach. There's a shop and pub in Llanengan, otherwise you'll have to go into

Abersoch for shops, food, cafes, etc. St Tudwals pub in Abersoch is where most young surfers drink. The local surf shop based in Abersoch will provide a local surf check on 0175871 2060 (see Appendix for address).

Accommodation   You can camp above the beach, but there are plenty of caravan parks and camp sites around Abersoch.

13 ABERDARON
➤ *Landranger 123, GR 172264*

Surf   A south-facing beach close to the end of the Lleyn Peninsula, with a beach break which is always considerably smaller than Hell's Mouth, but may be worth checking out if the surf's too big at the latter. It only breaks at high tide as the strong tidal race offshore cuts off the swell as the tide drops. N to NW winds are offshore.

Access   Aberdaron is well-signposted, and is at the end of the B4413. Park above the beach.

As hollow as it gets, Hell's Mouth

Facilities   Shops, pubs and cafes in Aberdaron. There are good views of Bardsey Island, two miles offshore. Boat trips to Bardsey leave from Aberdaron.

Accommodation   A number of caravan parks and camp sites.

14 PORTH OER / WHISTLING SANDS
➤ Landranger 123, GR 166300

Surf   A north west-facing beach which can get good waves when S winds are pushing a big swell round the peninsula to wrap into the beach. A good right-hander can be found off the sand bar in the middle of the beach breaking towards the cafe, although there are strong rips to be wary of near the rocks at this end of the beach. It's best just after high tide. S to SE winds are offshore. OK for beginners but it it can get very crowded. Surfing is restricted in the summer.

Access   There are various turnings from the B4413 to the hamlet of Methlem, and just to the south of the hamlet there's a turn-off to the beach. There'a a car park on the cliffs about 200 yards from the beach.

Facilities   Cafe on the beach in summer, toilets in the car park.

Accommodation   A number of caravan parks and camp sites.

15 PORTH COLMON / TRAETH PENLLECH
➤ Landranger 123, GR 200343

Surf   There are beach break peaks to be found on Traeth Penllech, and to the south there's a left-hander from swells wrapping round Penryn Golmon. Tends to be better on high tide, and as the tide is dropping. SE winds are offshore. OK for beginners.

Access   The beach is reached via a turn-off from the B4117 at Llangwnaddl. A steep path down a narrow valley leads to the beach. There's a coast path along the cliffs to the north of Traeth Penllech leading to a number of small sand and shingle coves.

Facilities   None.

Accommodation   Caravan parks and camp sites.

16 PORTH TOWYN
➤ Landranger 123, GR 230376

Surf   As with Whistling Sands, and Porth Colmon, Porth Towyn works when a S'ly wind pushes a big swell around onto the north coast of the peninsula. There's a good left-hander breaking off the rocks at the western end of the beach. It's best around low tide. S to SE winds are offshore. I understand there's also a wave to be had at Porth Ysgaden, immediately south of Porth Towyn.

Access   There are turn-offs to the beach from the B4417 just to the south of Tudweiliog.

Facilities   None - the nearest are in Tudweiliog.

Accommodation   See Porth Colmon.

17 PORTH DINLLAEN / MORFA NEFYN
➤ Landranger 123, GR 280410

Surf   A crescent of beach facing N to NW, which gets some shelter from W'ly winds. On a very big swell being pushed in by winds from S to W, the swell may wrap around the headland to give useful surf when most other beaches are no good. Best near high tide but on the ebb. Winds from W through to S are offshore.

Access   The B4412 runs off the A497 into Morfa Nefyn; there's a road to the beach at the NW end of the village.

Facilities   Shops, pubs, etc in Morfa Nefyn.

Accommodation   Caravan parks and camp sites locally; many more on the other side of the peninsula around Pwllheli and Abersoch.

18 PORTH NEVIN, NEFYN
➤ Landranger 123, GR 300410

Surf   A N to NW-facing beach which works on very big swells wrapping around from the west. There's a good left-hand point break off Penrhyn Nefyn headland, with W to SW winds being cross-shore/offshore here and holding up the face to give quite hollow waves at times. Not very consistent.

Access   The beach is easily reached from Nefyn, which is located at the junction of the A497 with the B4417.

Facilities Refreshments available in Nefyn.

Accommodation See Porth Dinllaen.

19 TREFOR
► *Landranger 123, GR 376474*

Surf A sand and shingle beach on the edge of a harbour, facing N, and enclosed by a short breakwater. There's a left-hand point break just outside the breakwater which needs a really massive swell for the waves to get up this far. When it does work it gives a good quality wave. It's not a break for inexperienced surfers though, as getting in and out of the water can be tricky, especially if the swell is big. S to SW winds are offshore.

Access Take the turn-off to Trefor from the A499 coast road at the point where it turns inland. There's a car park above the beach.

Facilities Shops etc. in the village.

Accommodation Caravan park and camp site just to the north east of the village, also see Porth Dinllaen.

20 PONTLLYFNI
► *Landranger 115, GR 430525*

Surf A W-facing boulder point producing long lefts on a big SW swell. It's best on a dropping tide, and in E to SE winds. There's a strong rip to the north, making it difficult to stay in the line-up. This, and the large rocks on the beach, make it unsuitable for beginners.

Access There's a turn-off to the beach from the A499, which is about 1/4 mile inland.

Facilities Shops in the village.

Accommodation Caravan park and camp site close to the beach.

21 DINAS DINLLE
► *Landranger 115, GR 465565*

Surf A long W to SW-facing shingle beach which can give peaks along its length from numerous offshore sandbanks. It needs a very big SW swell to produce a wave, and is usually at its best around mid tide, but doesn't often have good shape. E'ly winds

are offshore. Strong winds will easily spoil the waves. A good beach for beginners and windsurfers!

Access There are turn-offs from the A499 to the coast at Llandwrog.

Facilities Plenty above the beach. The nearest large town is Caernarfon eight miles to the north.

Accommodation Caravan parks and camp sites. There's a camp site in the village itself, and plenty more towards Caernarfon.

22 LLANDUDNO

Surf Llandudno is a popular holiday resort, and hardly known for the quality of its surf, but this N to NE-facing bay can produce a wave in strong NW or W winds. It usually only holds the swell for a day with the best waves being produced by fast-moving depressions. There's no rip to speak of, but the beach defences can be a hazard.

Access Llandudno is well-signposted from all the roads in the area. There's free parking along the promenade.

Facilities This is a really traditional British seaside resort, and has everything you'd expect from donkey rides to fish and chips, not to mention excellent views from the top of Great Orme Head at the west end of the bay. There is a local surf shop and club (see Appendix for details).

Accommodation There are plenty of caravan parks and camp sites to be found along this stretch of the coast. Youth hostels at Conwy and Mochdre.

23 RHOS-ON-SEA

Surf A NE-facing point break consisting of rocks and mussel beds which can have a good wave. It works in strong N to NW winds which produce long lefts. Strong rips on a rising tide make it surfable on the ebb tide only. There's an outside point which can hold bigger waves but it's dangerous due to the strength of the rip. Not suitable for beginners. The harbour entrance also breaks on larger swells and is less affected by the rip.

Access About two miles east of Llandudno, or if coming from the east, take the turn-off from the A55 at the signposted roundabout just west of Colwyn Bay.

Facilities   Plenty of refreshment facilities available in the town.

Accommodation   See Llandudno.

24 LLANDULAS BREAKWATER

Surf   A north-facing point break sheltered by the breakwater which works well in strong W winds and sometimes NW winds too. The shallow boulder point gives clean lefts, but a very strong rip makes for plenty of paddling in order to stay in the line-up. Not recommended for beginners.

Access   There's a roundabout on the A55 at Llandulas which gives access to the coast. You can check out the break from the road as you drive past.

Facilities   Shops and refreshments available in Llandulas or the nearby towns of Colwyn Bay and Abergele.

Accommodation   Plenty around Colwyn Bay and Llandudno. See Llandudno.

ANGLESEY AND HOLY ISLAND

From the Welsh mainland we now cross over the Menai Straits to Anglesey (Ynys Mon), and Holy Island (Ynys Gybi) via Thomas Telford's impressive suspension bridge. Once on Anglesey, you'll find that the A5 cuts diagonally across it to Holy Island and Holyhead.

As regards accommodation, I won't give details on each specific break - Anglesey isn't very big (276 sq.m.), and Holy Island is tiny, so wherever you stay you won't be far from any of the beaches mentioned here. There are caravan parks and camp sites dotted all over Anglesey, especially on the NE side.

The beaches are described as if travelling around the two islands in a clockwise direction, starting from the SW corner of Anglesey.

1 ABERFRRAW, ANGLESEY
➤ *Landranger 114, GR 355675*

Surf   A SW-facing beach and rivermouth break, which works best on a SW swell. There are long rights at the mouth of the Afon Ffraw, which have a good shape in light winds. NE winds are offshore. The beach breaks are best at the S end of the bay, with long rides off the rocky outcrops. It's a long

walk across the dunes to check it out, but it's often uncrowded. Safe for beginners - there is a slight rip running south along the beach, but it doesn't pose any real danger.

Access   The A4080 runs through Aberffraw, where you can park. There is a one mile walk to the beach.

Facilities   Aberffraw village has a pub and limited refreshment facilities.

2 CABLE BAY (PORTH TRECASTELL), ANGLESEY
➤ *Landranger 114, GR 334707*

Surf   A narrow, W-facing bay which produces good waves on most SW or W swells. It can hold a good-sized wave and is best around mid tide. NE winds are offshore. There's a strong rip along the southern headland which experienced surfers will find useful for paddling out, but beginners should keep away from. It is very popular with canoeists. So expect the usual hassles.

Access   Three miles north of Aberffraw on the A4080. There's a car park above the beach.

Facilities   Snack bar in the car park in summer, otherwise the nearest shops are at Llanfeilog or Rhosneigr, a couple of miles to the north.

3 RHOSNEIGR, ANGLESEY
➤ *Landranger 114, GR 320730*

Surf   Rhosneigr has two beaches; Traeth Llydan to the south of the town, and Traeth Crigyll to the north, which in turn passes into Traeth Cymyran to the north again. All of them face SW, and work on a SW or W swell. There are peaks in the middle of both Traeth Llydan and Traeth Crigyll and you may find an occasional left off the rocks of Carreglydan at the south end of Traeth Llydan. Less frequent is a right off the rocks at the north end of the beach.

Winds from N through to E are offshore. All the beaches are pretty safe for beginners on smaller swells, but there's a rip by the river mouth at the southern end of Traeth Crigyll.

Access   Traeth Llydan and Traeth Crigyll are easily reached from Rhosneigr, which is on the A4080. Access to Traeth Cymran is not so easy, and involves either a long walk north from Rhosneigr, or a walk south via the hamlet of Llanfairyneubwll.

Facilities Plenty of shops and pubs in Rhosneigr; there's a caravan park and camp site above Traeth Crigyll.

4 SILVER BAY, HOLY ISLAND
➤ *Landranger 114, GR 291753*

Surf A small, south-facing bay which works when the beaches to the south are onshore. The headland to the west forces SW winds offshore producing good hollow waves at mid to low tide. The lefts at the eastern end of the bay break over large rocks making it unsuitable for inexperienced surfers, but the other waves in the bay are OK.

Access Take the B4546 turn-off from the A5 and cross over to Holy Island on the Four Mile Bridge. From here head to Rhoscolyn. Access to the beach is via the caravan site, but you will find this shut out of season. You can also walk up to Silver Bay from Traeth Cymyran.

Facilities None.

5 TREARDDUR BAY, HOLY ISLAND
➤ *Landranger 114, GR 256790*

Surf A small sandy SW-facing beach which doesn't work very often, but can hold waves when Rhosneigr and Cable Bay are blown out. It's very popular with boardsailers and canoeists.

Access The town of Trearddur is on the B4245, and is almost equidistant between the two bridges from Anglesey to Holy Island so it doesn't really matter which of them you take to get there. Park above the bay.

Facilities Shops, pubs, etc. in nearby Trearddur. There are a number of camp sites in the area.

6 PORTH SWTAN (CHURCH BAY), ANGLESEY
➤ *Landranger 115, GR 300804*

Surf A west-facing bay which works best when strong NW winds have pushed a swell in. There are lefts off the rocky ledges at the south end of the bay, and a peak in the middle which gives rights. It's not very consistent, but sheltered from SW winds, and may be worth checking on a big swell if other beaches are onshore.

Access Porth Swtan is on Anglesey's NW coast, and is reached via a turn-off from the A5025 to Rhydwyn, from where the beach is signposted. There's a car park above the beach.

Facilities Pub and toilets above the beach. Camp site.

7 TRAETH LLIGWY, ANGLESEY
➤ *Landranger 115, GR 495875*

Surf A NE-facing bay which has peaks along it after a strong NW or N gale has been blowing. SW winds are offshore here. OK for beginners.

Access There's a turn off to Traeth Lligwy from the A5025 at Brynrefail, just N of Rhos Lligwy, or from the Moelfre roundabout to the south. Parking is available above the beach.

Facilities Refreshment caravan and public toilets in car park.
There are other beaches on Anglesey that I understand have surf, but on which I could get no definite up-to-date information.

LLANDWYN ISLAND (Landranger 115, GR 385625) There are waves to be had on either side of the 'island' (it is in fact a promontory) in Llandwyn Bay and Malltreath Bay, and also a left and right off the N and S side of the island respectively. To get there take the A4080 from Llanfairpwllgwyngyll to Niwbrch (Newborough), from where there's a track through the forest to the beach.

PORTH NOBLA (Landranger 115, GR330711) Apparently there are a number of breaks to be had here - beach, reef, and point, so it sounds like an ideal spot for all standards of surfer. The bay is actually a southern extension of Rhosneigr's Traeth Llydan. It's just off the A4080, and there's parking above the beach.

BENLLECH BAY (Landranger 115, GR 525825) A NE-facing beach which has beach break waves on a heavy swell from the north, usually only in the winter months. SW winds are offshore. OK for beginners. Benllech is Anglesey's main holiday town and is easily reached on the A5025.

12 THE SEVERN BORE

The Severn Bore is unquestionably the longest wave in Britain - in fact it's one of the longest surfable waves in the world. It's just unfortunate that it happens to be up a river rather than on a beach.

However if the idea of surfing on a river takes your fancy, here's a chance to ride a wave for a mile or more if conditions are favourable.

The Bore is a tidal wave that's channelled up the river Severn at a speed of around 10mph on certain spring tides. It can vary in height from a few inches to around head high, depending on the prevailing conditions. Both wind strength and direction and the amount of water flowing down the river have a marked effect upon the height of the wave.

The wave is usually surfed between Newnham and Lower Partington, where the river forks. There are several points of access. As the wave approaches you'll here a roar downstream, until it eventually appears around a bend in the river as a wall of water flowing upstream. This is an impressive sight if the wave's big.

Once you're up and riding, there are a number of factors to consider that don't apply on an ocean wave. You must decide which side of the wave will fade away (as it frequently does), be aware of the backwash from the river bank, and remember that the bends in the river will also affect the shape of the wave. All this makes surfing the Severn bore an interesting experience. You'll find that the kind of wetsuit you're wearing at your local break at the particular time of year you decide to surf the Bore should be sufficient for the temperature of the river water.

There's no way of knowing for an absolute certainty just how big the wave will be, but the National Rivers Authority provide a leaflet giving information on dates, times, and prospects for the Bore for each year, which is well worth getting hold of if you intend to surf here (the address is in the Appendix).

Largest bores occur on tides over 32ft with wave height at the bank being bigger than in mid-stream.

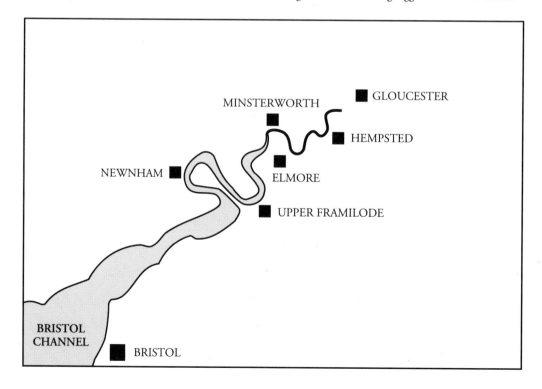

These occur at the equinox, and 1-3 days after full
and new moons. The Severn Bore is officially the
longest wave ever ridden. The present record is 2.5
miles by David Partington on September 27th 1988.

There are several access points along the river; but
make sure you're not trespassing before you start
lugging your board across someone's field. It's also
worth arriving well before the wave is due, especially
at week-ends or holidays when local traffic
congestion can be severe.

The access points given here are from the river
mouth, going upstream.

NEWNHAM - Situated on the west bank of the
river, on the A48 Gloucester-Chepstow road. There's
access to the river in Newnham and half a mile
further north on the A48 at BROADOAK. Both
spots are quite shallow, with a deeper channel on the
west bank - bear the water depth in mind if/when
you wipe out!

FRAMILODE - On the east bank half a mile N of
the village of Saul on the B4071. Framilode is just
off the A38 Gloucester-Bristol road and close to
junction 13 on the M5. Deeper water by the east
bank.

EPNEY - One mile upriver of Framilode. Deeper
water by the east bank. Note that the deepwater
channel narrows considerably 400 yards north.

WEST BANK - From the Bird in Hand pub north
to Minsterworth, the A48 runs along the river bank
for about 1.5 miles. You can take off anywhere along
this stretch, which is one of the favourite take-off
points. Most of the land and access points to the
river are private so you should keep to the public
footpath along the riverbank.

ELMORE BACK - Another good take-off point: on
the opposite side of the river from Minsterworth.

ELMORE AND STONEBENCH - Stonebench is
at the marked southerly meander in the river, just off
the A38, with Elmore just beyond. You drive
through Elmore for Elmore Back.

REA - Close to the village of Hempsted, which is
south of Gloucester on the A430. The river here is
straight for about a mile before making a long
sweeping bend to the right. This is one of the best
places to take off. A good ride could get you all the
way to Lower Partington, two miles to the north.

13 WAVES & SURF

Here's a very brief look at the way in which waves and surf are produced.

A wave coming out of deep water into the shallow water of a beach or reef will be travelling at about 15 to 20mph and will start to 'drag' on the sea floor. This shortens its wave length, which in turn increases the steepness of the wave, tending to make it less stable.

This is the prelude to the wave breaking, which will eventually occur in water that has a depth of about 1.3 times the wave height, so you could expect to find a 6ft wave breaking in water just over 4.5ft deep - in theory. This may not always be the case.

The energy released by a breaking wave is phenomenal - large waves have been recorded exerting a force of 6,000 pounds per square foot in the surf, or impact zone; so it's hardly surprising that a bad wipeout can be such an memorable experience! Once a wave breaks, it will generally take one of three forms; surging, spilling, or plunging.

SURGING WAVES - These are of little use to surfers. They come in out of relatively deep water on to steep beaches, and rather than break, surge up the beach. You may witness this on some surf beaches at high tide when the profile of the beach becomes too steep to enable the wave to break properly.

SPILLING WAVES - The most common type to be found on British beaches. They are produced by a gently sloping sea bed, which causes the wave to peak gradually: the release of energy from the wave is relatively slow, so the crest 'spills' down the wave face.

PLUNGING WAVES - These are the spectacular waves of which the surfing magazines are full. Good examples are Pipeline in Hawaii and Thurso East in Scotland. Plunging waves are more likely to occur at reef breaks than on beaches.

TYPES OF BREAK

In Britain beach breaks are far and away the most commonly surfed waves, with occasional reef and point breaks dotted around the coastline. Beach breaks tend not to have the power of reef breaks. Point breaks, where the wave may break over a sand or rock bottom (or both), often give longer rides. A good point break may wrap around a headland and

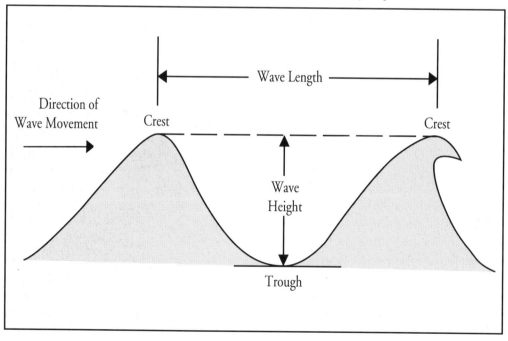

run into a bay for hundreds of yards. Usually, it is more mellow than the fast and heavy wave commonly found on reef breaks.

BEACH BREAKS - Beach break waves occur at their best where a well-defined sand or gravel bar has formed, causing waves to break over it as they move in from deep water in a distinct peak that ideally peels both left and right. As the sand that makes up these bars is readily shifted by currents and wave action, they may change shape frequently. Because of this it does not always follow that a beach that has a good reputation for surf will ALWAYS have good waves. If the bars are in bad shape you may find the waves backing off (when the water is slightly too deep to allow the wave to break), or closing out (when the entire length of the wave face hits a long section of beach of the same depth and breaks simultaneously).

Once the wave has broken and rushed up the beach, the water has to drain back out to sea. It does so in rip channels, which are often readily discernible as channels of choppy but unbroken water in between areas of surf. The flow of water out to sea in these channels can be surprisingly powerful in large surf, and although they provide an easy means of

getting out to the breaking waves for experienced surfers, beginners should treat them with respect. If you do get caught in a rip, DON'T try to swim or paddle against it: head off at right angles to it, and you should soon find yourself out of the channel of seaward flowing water. You may now find yourself directly in the path of oncoming walls of white water, but at least these will push you shorewards again.

Apart from the easily-avoided hazard of rip currents, beach breaks provide ideal and generally safe waves on which to learn to surf.

REEF BREAKS - A reef break will occur where any underwater obstruction rises suddenly above the sea floor, causing waves to peak and break over it. In Britain it will invariably be a rock formation - usually a rock shelf, such as at Thurso East, Porthleven, Staithes, and Kimmeridge. In some cases you may even get a reef break over a submerged wreck.

This is where you're most likely to find plunging breakers, or in surfspeak, tubes. As the swell moves shoreward out of deep water, it will come up against the reef which obstructs its forward movement. The swell appears to 'trip' over the reef, producing a peak that jacks up abruptly, throwing the lip way out in

Idealised weather chart for North Atlantic inducing potentially excellent surf conditions for the west coast of Britain and Europe The high over Europe creates calm, settled weather with gentle offshore breezes, and may become sufficiently well established to 'block' the depression in mid-Atlantic, thus preventing it from moving over the country, but allowing the swell from the intense storm activity to move unhindered towards the British Isles. If you see a chart looking anything like this, drop everything and head for the coast.

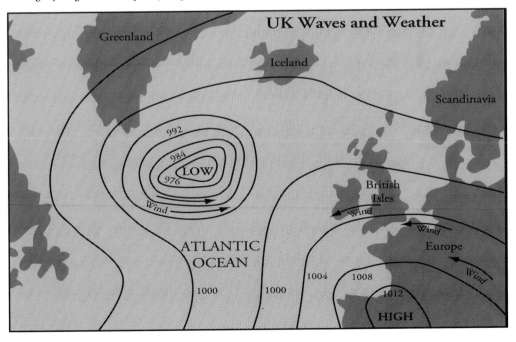

front of the face. Under ideal conditions it peels off rapidly left and/or right to give a fast, hollow, and often heavy wave. This is accentuated by an offshore wind.

The speed and power of the wave is a result of all the energy of the swell being dispersed quickly and over a small area as the wave breaks. A wipeout on a reef break often means a hard and rocky landing for both board and rider. These are obviously not the waves for beginners to start experimenting upon.

POINT BREAKS - Good examples are not too common in Britain, but a quality point break is often well worth travelling for. One good example is at Lynmouth in Devon, a left-hander which only really works regularly in winter. Under ideal conditions a swell hitting a promontory or headland will 'wrap around' this natural projection, often with almost machine-like regularity and evenness between waves. The wave may break first over a rock or boulder bottom which becomes sand as the wave moves into the bay. As the wave moves into shallow water, it may close-out due to this build-up of sand on the inside of the bay.

Not covered under these three headings are rivermouth breaks, which occur in estuaries as a result of the depositing of sand by the slow-moving river as it reaches the end of its journey. These are often nothing more than beach breaks over a sand bar, but it's often necessary to beware of strong seaward currents from the river flowing out to sea, particularly on a dropping tide or after heavy rainfall.

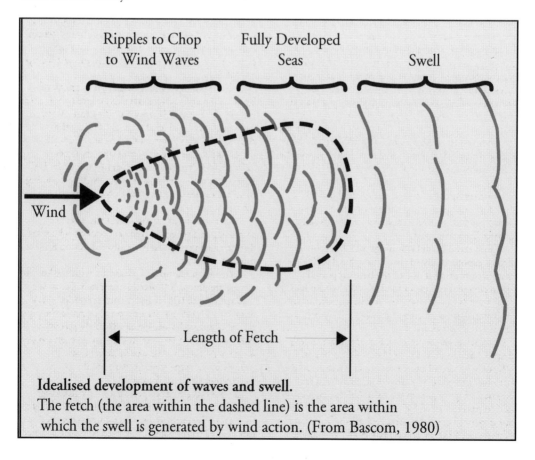

Idealised development of waves and swell.
The fetch (the area within the dashed line) is the area within which the swell is generated by wind action. (From Bascom, 1980)

14 GREEN SEAS & SAS

After having travelled around virtually the whole of the coastline of England, Scotland and Wales to research this book I was left in little doubt that for such a small island the British Isles has some of the most varied and attractive coastline you could ever hope to surf.

However, in many cases that beauty was only skin deep, as serious pollution problems could be found almost everywhere I went - sewage in Cornwall and Yorkshire; toxic waste in South Wales; an oil spill in Devon; and clapped-out cars and farm machinery dumped on beaches in the Outer Hebrides were just a few examples.

As surfers we're probably more exposed than any other water users to the harmful effects of water and beach pollution, so we should think ourselves lucky that in recent years we've had one of the most effective of grass-roots environmental groups campaigning on our behalf in the form of Surfers Against Sewage. If you surf - even if it's only for a week or two each year - you should become a member of SAS, as it's in your interest and that of our coastline, which is, after all, the only one we've got.

To give you some idea of what SAS are all about, Chris Hines, SAS General Secretary, has put together a few words for `Surf UK'.

`Surfers Against Sewage was formed in 1990 by a group of St. Agnes-based surfers who were quite literally sick of surfing in sewage-polluted waters on Cornwall's north coast.

From those small beginnings SAS has grown almost exponentially so that it now has 16,000 members, making it one of the best supported environmental groups in the UK. We've also had great success in attracting the media's attention to our campaigns, featuring regularly on TV, radio and in the national newspapers.

But, what are we fighting for, and how? Well, despite having some 11,000 kms of coastline in the UK, only a third of our recreational beaches have been designated by the Government as `bathing beaches'. Eighty percent of these 457 beaches are said to pass the 1976 EC Bathing Water Directive, but they only meet the bare legal minimum standard of two out of the 19 criteria laid down by the EC.

The rest don't even manage this.

Non-designated beaches are not monitored, so that for many of the sites where our members surf no-one even knows what the water contains - but with over 300 million gallons of raw or virtually untreated sewage being discharged around the UK coastline EVERY DAY it's not hard to guess - and it's also not hard to guess why so many of our members complain of illnesses after surfing at certain locations.

In addition, even designated beaches are only monitored in summer, yet with the development of the wetsuit many surfers and other water users are in the sea all year round.

The tests themselves are known to be inadequate, as they only test for coliforms (these can cause upset stomachs and ear nose and throat infections) which only survive for a couple of hours in salt water. Human pathogens, such as hepatitis, can last for up to 100 days.

What SAS are campaigning for is to get all of Britain's beaches up to a standard where they would pass all 19 of the EC directives. The real answer to sewage disposal is to discharge an effluent that is clean in the outfall pipe. This can be achieved by applying full primary and secondary treatment followed by ultra-violet light disinfection. The UV breaks down the DNA of the viruses thus rendering them incapable of replication. This is known as `tertiary treatment'.

Another form of tertiary treatment that is showing good potential is microfiltration where the disease causing organisms are filtered out on a microscopic scale.

Jersey is an example of a location with the kind of sewage treatment SAS would eventually like to see throughout the UK - a full treatment works to UV standard. This results in a bacterial count in the pipe that is a hundred times cleaner than the standard that the Government requires to give a beach a pass - hence SAS' line that we would rather bathe in Jersey's outfall pipe than on many of the Government's passed beaches!

By pursuing cases of personal injury resulting from polluted waters through legal avenues SAS are increasing the pressure on water companies to adopt this type of technology. Only then will they be able to absolve themselves of responsibility.

SAS also argue strongly, supported by facts and figures, that full treatment is cheaper than the old pump and dump mentality of partially long sea outfalls.

As a measure of how seriously SAS are taken we were called in front of the House of Lords to give evidence on the revision of the 1976 EC Bathing Water Directive.

For a very young and relatively small organisation SAS has so far received a tremendous level of support, achieved a very high media profile and been extremely successful in raising public awareness of these issues. But we still need all the support we can get. Anyone who uses the sea for recreational purposes should consider joining SAS, as we campaign on behalf of ALL recreational water users and not just surfers.

Britain's coastline is undoubtedly very special; it's waves can be surprisingly good; let's work together to ensure that they're also clean.'

Although I've tried to include details on every aspect of the surf at each location mentioned in the guide, I'm afraid you won't find much on water quality. This is not a cop-out - I had plenty of data available to me, but at many beaches this is constantly changing depending on improvement work (or lack of), and I felt that during the life of this book the details could easily become out of date and inaccurate, so it wasn't really worth including them.

The best way to ensure reasonably up-to-date information on water quality around the British coastline is to get hold of a copy of the Marine Conservation Society's 'Good Beach Guide', which is published annually. Whilst it won't cover every break mentioned in this book, it's as detailed a guide to water quality as you'll find, and it also provides interesting details on the various beach awards that are on offer these days. Suffice to say, a beach award flag flying above your local break is not necessarily a guarantee that the water is sewage or pollution free.

SURFERS AGAINST SEWAGE , THE OLD COUNTHOUSE WAREHOUSE, WHEAL KITTY, ST. AGNES, CORNWALL TR5 0RE Tel. 01872 553001 Fax. 01872 552615

THE MARINE CONSERVATION SOCIETY, 9 GLOUCESTER ROAD, ROSS-ON-WYE, HEREFORDSHIRE HR9 5BU Tel. 01989 566017 Fax. 01989 567815

15 APPENDIX: SURF DATA

Surfing in Britain is controlled by the British Surfing Association. Membership of the BSA is open to all surfers, would-be surfers, even non-surfers, who may join direct, or as members of affiliated clubs (the BSA will be able to tell you which is your nearest surf club).

The BSA is recognised by the British Sports Council, and the English, Welsh, Scottish, and Channel Islands Surfing Federations are affiliated to the Association.

Members receive a membership card and a periodic newsletter with news of developments in the sport both at home and abroad. The newsletter often contains special offers on equipment for members. A number of surf shops offer discount to BSA mambers.

Members also receive, on request, public liability insurance at specially negotiated rates, and are sent entry forms to BSA-organised surfing contests (which include the GB, English, Welsh, and Scottish Nationals, the British Cup, the GB Schools, GB Students championships, and the GB Inter-Club championships).

Further details can be obtained from Colin Wilson, British Surfing Association, Champions Yard, Penzance, Cornwall TR18 2SS (Tel and Fax 01736 60250).

SURF MAGAZINES

British surfing magazines have tended to have an ephemeral existence in the past, although with the increasing popularity of the sport those that exist at present will hopefully be with us for some time to come.

WAVELENGTH is the best established. It's published bi-monthly, although this may be extended by a few weeks in the quieter winter months. All good surf shops and most large newsagents in the UK will stock it. Also available from Wavelength Magazine, 6d Treloggar Industrial Estate, Newquay, Cornwall, TR7 2SK.

SURF magazine first appeared in 1989, rising from the ashes of SURF SCENE. Publication at the time of writing seems to be rather erratic, with no obvious publication dates, although it does appear a number of times each year. All good surf shops and newsagents will stock it or contact Stone Leisure Group, Andrew House, 2a Granville Road, Sidcup, Kent DA14 4BN.

CARVE is the most recent addition to the scene. Carve first appeared in 1994. Available at most surf shops and newsagents, or by subscription from Orca Publications, 11 Cliff Road, Newquay, Cornwall, TR7 2NE. BSA members get subscriptions at a slightly discounted rate.

PIPELINE NEWS is the official SAS newsletter, free to members and 50p to non members.

TUBE NEWS is the magazine of the Wessex Surf Club, and is Britain's longest running surf magazine. It's more parochial than the two national magazines and deals mainly with the south coast. Some surf shops may stock it otherwise contact Wessex Surf Club, c/o 19 Stalham Road, Branksome, Poole, Dorset.

SURF'S UP is a low-key magazine aimed at east coast surfers, so it may well contain useful information for London-based surfers. The editor, Paul Knowles, should be able to supply you with a copy. Write to him at 2, Frognall Cottages, Wickhambreaux, Canterbury, Kent CT3 1SB

SURF REPORTS

WAVECALL SURF PREDICTIONS
0891 212 plus
098 Scotland
097 Wales
096 East Coast
095 South West
094 South Coast

SURFCALL SURF REPORT
0839 505 plus
698 - Scotland
697 - Wales
696 - East Coast
695 - South West
694 - South Coast

SURFLINE SURF REPORT
Gower Peninsula - 0891 445445

BIG G'S SURF REPORT
0336 406 plus
861 - Scotland
862 - East Coast
863 - South Coast
864 - South West
865 - Wales

SURF CHECK
Saltburn area - 0891 545543

SEVERN BORE   To obtain information on times
and dates that the Bore appears, contact the
National Rivers Authority, Sapphire East, 550
Streetsbrook Road, Solihull B91 1QT (0121 711
2324). Further information on the Bore can be
found in 'The Severn Bore', by F.W. Rowbotham
(published by David and Charles).

SELECTED COASTAL SURF SHOPS, AS OF AUTUMN 1994

SCOTLAND

Granite Reef 45 Justice Street Aberdeen
01224 621193

Clan 45 Hyndland Street Partick Glasgow
0141 339 6523

Mach 1146 Argyle Street Glasgow
0141 334 5559

Mach 4 Lady Lawson Street Edinburgh
0131 229 5887

ESP Shepherd's Close 50a High Street Elgin
01343 550129

Good Vibes Surf Shop 21 Sinclair Street Thurso
01847 63312

NORTH EAST ENGLAND / YORKSHIRE

Sandy's Surf Shop 39 Front Street North Shields
0191 296 3049

Sharksports Ltd Nordstrom House North Broomhill
Morpeth
01670 760365

Saltburn Surf Shop Lower Promenade Saltburn-by-
the-Sea
01287 624023

Secret Spot Surf Shop 4 Pavilion Terrace Scarborough 01723 500467	Scarborough's leading watersports specialists, with full range of wetsuits, surfboards & accessories

Killerby Park Surf Shop Cayton Bay Scarbough YO11 3NR 01723 582495 (Surf Report)	Excellent surfing shop at car park, open every day in season with snack food and free hot showers

NDR' Easter Surfboards Unit E J.T Atkinson Ind.
Estate Bury Road Hartlepool
01429 261119

EAST ANGLIA

Boardtalk 1 Battery Green Road Lowestoft
01502 517992   *49.99*

King Watersports & Leisure 16 The Street Blundeston Lowestoft 01502 730182	Open 7 days a week, Surf equipment & Padi Scuba Diving Centre

SOUTH COAST

K Bay Longboards 20 Marlborough Place
Wimborne Dorset
01202 881322

Alpine Waves 2 Lagland Street Poole
01202 665533

French Connection 4 Banks Road Sandbanks Poole
01202 707757

Hardcore Surf Sunseeker Marina West Quay Road
Poole
01202 675672

Impact Watersports 439 Poole Road Branksome
Poole
01202 765551

Oceanos 60 Panarama Road Sandbanks Poole
01202 701559

Bournemouth Surfing Centre 127 Belle Vue Road
Southbourne Bournemouth
01202 433544

Hot Rocks Surf Shop 214-216 Old Christchurch
Road Bournemouth
01202 293834

Southsea Surf Shop Langstone Marina Fort
Cumberland Road Southsea
01705 861555

Shore Watersports Shore Road East Wittering
01243 672315

Shore Watersports Northney Marina Hayling Island
0705 467334

Surf Connection 264 Sea Front Hayling Island
01705 467417

Vitamin Sea Surfboards Unit D/5 West End Garage
Station Road Hayling Island
01705 468822

Surfladle Surf Shop Ferry Road Shoreham Beach
01273 465366

Oceansports 368 Kingsway Hove
01273 420142

Surf Hog 7 Aldwick Road Bognor Regis
01243 867945

Surf Shack Market Road Rye
01797 225746

DEVON

Freebird Surfboards Chivenor Ind. Estate Chivenor
Braunton
01271 813554

Second Skin Surf Shop 4 Caen Street Braunton
01271 812195

Laser Surfboards Dennis Ind. Estate Knowle
Braunton
01271 816986

Legends Surf Shop 2 West Cross Caen Street
Braunton
01271 817889

Mango Surf Shop 4 West Cross Caen Street
Braunton
01271 816227

Tiki Surf Shop Caen Shopping Centre Braunton
01271 815757

Circle One Wet Suits Marsh Lane Lords Meadow
Ind Estate Crediton
01363 773005

Salt Rock Surf Shop 24 Saunton Road Braunton
01271 815306

Ra Wetsuits 58 South Street Braunton
01271 814716

Bay Surf Shop 3 Barton Court Barton Road
Woolacombe
01271 870961

Two Bare Feet 15 Torwood Street Torquay
01803 296734

Harbour Sports The Harbour Paignton
01803 550180

Harbour Sports The Barbican Plymouth
01752 660604

Surfing Life 154 Cornwall Street Plymouth
01752 668774

CORNWALL

Surf Wind 'n' Ski Bristol & West House 27a Belle
Vue Bude
01288 356156

Zuma Jays Surf Shop Belle Vue Lane Bude
01288 354956

Ann's Cottage Surf Shop Old Polzeath
01208 862162

North Shore Surf Shop 36 Fore Street Newquay TR7 1LP 01637 850620 (Surf Report)	Excellent surfing shop with professional forecast available

Surfside Polzeath Beach
01208 863426
and The Parade Polzeath
01208 862002

Boardwalk Surf Shop 17 Cliff Road Newquay
01637 878880

Newquay Surfboard Company 3 Wesley Yards
Newquay
01637 850881

The Board Room 6 Alma Place Newquay
01637 878790

Custard Point Quarry Park Road Newquay
01637 878232

Natural Flight Surfboards The Workshops Penmure
Close Trenance Hill Newquay
01637 879465

Pirate Surfboards The Workshops Trenance Road
Newquay
01637 872186

Rocky Point Surf Designs 5 Beach Road Newquay
01637 871169

Wavekraft Unit 9b Treloggan Industrial Estate
Newquay
01637 877629

Fistral Surf Co 1 Beacon Road Newquay
01637 876169
also at 19 Cliff Road Newquay
01637 850378
also at Kenwyn Street Truro
01872 260850

Aggie Surfshop Peterville St. Agnes
01872 553818

Armstrong Wetsuits The Quay Eddystone Road
Wadebridge
01208 814919

Big Wednesday 26 Church Street Falmouth
01326 211159

Constantine Bay Surf Store Constantine Bay St.
Merryn
01841 520250

Ocean Sports 17 West End Pentewan St. Austell
01726 842817

Polkerris Wetsuits 15 Polkerris Beach Par nr. Fowey
01726 815142

Praa Sands Surf Shop The Post Office Praa Sands
01736 763475

Surf Asylum 15 Kenwyn Street Truro
01872 225355

Tubes Surf Shop 16 Turf Street Bodmin
01208 78802

Westcountry Watersports 63 Fairmantle Street
Truro
01872 75342

Down The Line Market Square Arcade
Copperhouse Hayle
01736 757025

Ministry of Surf Unit 9 Trevassack Hill Hayle
01736 753967

Wet Suits Unlimited Princes Row Pensilva Liskeard
01579 63444

SOUTH WALES & THE GOWER

Gower Surf Company 667 Gower Road Upper
Killay Swansea
01792 297276

PJ's Surf Shop Llangennith Gower
01792 386669

Dave Friar Surf Shop 1 Chapel Street Mumbles
Swansea
01792 368861

Surf A Go-Go Acorn Country Stores Gower Road
Upper Killay Swansea
01792 204818

Wave Graffiti Penclawdd Trading Estate Penclawdd
Swansea
01792 850137

Mumbles Surf Shop 520 Mumbles Road Mumbles
Swansea
01792 368611

Surf Atlantic 6 Blodwen Terrace Penclawdd Swansea
01792 850863

Impact Surf Factory Unit 3 Fenton Yard Fenton
Place Porthcawl
01656 784456

Session Surfboards Unit 8 South Cornelly Trading
Estate Nr. Bridgend Mid Glamorgan
01656 744691

Black Rock Surf Shop 75 New Road Porthcawl
01656 782220

Continental Surf 87 Main Roadm Ogmore-by-Sea
01656 880549

Porthcawl Marine 20 New Road Porthcawl
01656 784785

City Surf Shop 27 Castle Street Cardiff
01222 342068

PEMBROKESHIRE AREA

Haven Sports Marine Road Broad Haven
Haverfordwest
01437 781354

Seaweed Surf Shop Wilton House Quay Street
Haverfordwest
01437 760774

Waves n' Wheels Commons Road Pembroke
01646 622066

Ma Simes Surf Hut Cross Square St. Davids
01437 720433

Newsurf Surf Shop Newgale Filling Station Newgale Haverfordwest 01437 721398	Hire & sale of all your surfing gear, from the shop on the beach. Surf report - 01437 720698

West Coast Custom Wetsuits The Workshop Grove
Hill Pembroke
01646 686419

Surf Centre Ltd The Salterns Tenby
01834 845111

Underground Surf Shop 4 Church Street Tenby
01834 844234

Surf Centre Station Yard Station Road St. Clears
Dyfed
01994 231106

MID AND NORTH WALES

Breakaway Watersports The Surf Shop New Quay
Dyfed
01545 560169

Abersoch Surf Co The Bridge Abersoch Gwynedd LL53 7DY 01758 712365	One of the best ranges in the north west of surfboards & clothing. Also hire of surf, boogie boards & wetsuits

West Coast Surf Abersoch Outdoors The Square
Abersoch
01758 712060

Kaya Surf Mel's Yard Builder Street Llandudno
01492 581762

Tribal Connection 6 Castle Courtyard Castle Street
Llangollen Clwyd
01978 860160

Llandudno surf club - Eyri Riders contact Terry
Evans
01248 602521

BRITISH SURFING ASSOCIATION APPROVED SURF SCHOOLS

Outdoor Adventure Richard Gill Atlantic Court
Widemouth Bay Bude Cornwall EX23 0DF
01288 361312

Offshore Surfing Roger Mansfield 2 Oakleigh
Terrace Newquay Cornwall
01637 877083

National Surfing Centre Fistral Beach Newquay c/o
British Surfing Association Champions Yard
Penzance Cornwall TR18 2TA
01736 60250

Welsh National Surfing Centre Linda Sharp 71
Fairway Aberavon Port Talbot W. Glamorgan
01639 886246

Surfrider Activity Holidays Steve Rosenbaum The
Waters Fall Hotel Beach Road Woolacombe Devon
EX34 7AD
01271 870365

Skern Lodge Outdoor Centre Appledore Bideford
Devon EX39 1NG
01237 421203

PGL Young Adventure Tim Whalley Beam House
Torrington Devon EX38 8JF
01805 22992

Adventure International Chris Wilson Belle Vue
Bude Cornwall
01288 355551

Twr-y-Felin Outdoor Centre St. Davids
Pembrokeshire Dyfed Wales SA62 6QS
01437720391

Freetime Surfing Holidays Runnelstone Cottages St Levan Penzance TR19 6LU 01736 871 302 (Brochure available)	British Surfing Association approved surf school for surfing holidays, surf courses & introductory surfing sessions with qualified instruction, all equipment is supplied

BRITISH SURFING ASSOCIATION AFFILIATED SURF CLUBS

ENGLAND

Cornwall

St. Mawgan Waveriders Nick Morgan c/o OPS
WG, RAF St. Mawgan

Newquay Boardriders Neil Harris 23 Edgecumbe
Gardens Newquay
01637 875853

Sennen Surf Club Jon Matthews 2 Guival Cross
Guival Penzance

South Coast

Isle of Wight Club Ceri Williams 5 Rew Close
Ventnor
01983 866269

Wessex Surf Club Richard Simkins R.V.M. Flat 4
Otterbourne 5-7 Surrey Road Bournemouth Dorset
01202 752029

Ordnance Survey Duncan Gibson 14 Lawn Road
Portswood Southampton
01703 555720

Shore Surf Club Tim Orrell South Kives Cottage 65
Bognor Road Merston Chichester W. Sussex
01243 530325

South West

South West Pipeshredders Mike Saunders 7
Chambon Close Mimety Malmesbury Wilts.
01666 860489

Chapter Hotdoggers Dave Smy The Bungalow
North Devon College Old Sticklepath Hill
Barnstaple
01271 388114

Woolacombe Boardriders Craig Jepson Parklyn
Exeter Road Braunton
01271 816024

Croyde Surf Club Claire Dodds 4 Dyers Close Braunton
01271 815941

Other Areas

London Surf Club Stuart Morrisey 393 Peterborough Road Carshalton Surrey
0181 715 6981

Nottingham Surf Club Frank Ellis Almond Lodge 41 Sherwin Road Lenton Nottingham
01602 703002

Wales

Eryri Boardriders T J Evans 19 Fordd-y-Mynydd Llanllechid Gwynedd
01248 602521
Tywyn Surf Club Tony Jeffs Sunnyside Cottage Church Street Barmouth Gwynedd
01341 281059

Welsh Coast Surf Club Mike Shilling 88a Victoria Avenue Porthcawl Mid Glamorgan
0656 716250

Pembrokeshire Surf Club Chris Paine The Gables Church Road Haverfordwest
0437 710561

Langland Boardriders John Hutton 19 Croftfield Crescent Newton Swansea
0792 366104

Gower Bay Surf Club Dave Friar Dave Friar Surf Shop 1Chapel Street Mumbles Swansea
0792 368861

Gower Lifeguards Johhny Kapec 7 Beechwood Road Uplands Swansea
0792 474008

Channel Coast Surf Club Steve Lethbridge 6 Tresilian Close Llantwit Major South Glamorgan
0446 796547

NATIONAL SURFING FEDERATIONS

English Surfing Federation Alan Beard Toad Hall 18 Old Bridge Street Truro Cornwall

Welsh Surfing Federation Linda Sharp 71 Fairway Aberavon Port Talbot West Glamorgan
0639 886246

Scottish Surfing Federation Jason Simpson 44 Queen's Terrace Thurso Caithness

Other surf books from Fernhurst

The History of Surfing (Second Edition) *by Nat Young*

A magnificent, inspiring history of the sport. The 224 pages have 312 colour photos plus 252 black-and-white pictures. Nat Young, a former world champion, traces surfing's development from its origins among the Hawaiian kings to todays spectacular rides from the top professionals.

Surfing Fundamentals by *Nat Young*

Learn to ride the waves with this lively, colourful guide. Part 1 teaches basic surfing. Part 2 shows how to master the big stuff, make advanced manoeuvres and win competitions. Part 3 covers alternative ways of riding waves: Malibu boards, kneeboarding, wave skis and boogie boards.

Fernhurst Books are available from all good bookshops and chandleries. In case of difficulty, or if you would like a copy of our full catalogue, please send your name and address to:

Fernhurst Books, Duke's Path, High Street, Arundel, West Sussex BN18 9AJ